Rice, Rats and Rickshaws

Valerie Astill

An environmentally friendly book printed and bound in England by
www.printondemand-worldwide.com

Valerie Astill

www.fast-print.net/store.php

Rice, Rats and Rickshaws

A catalogue record for this book is available from the British Library

ISBN 978-178035-593-1

First published 2013 by
FASTPRINT PUBLISHING
Peterborough, England.

Rice, Rats and Rickshaws

A tour through China from Hong Kong to Beijing

via the provinces of Guangdong, Guangxi, Yunnan, Sichuan and Shaanxi

This is the account of a holiday in China in 1993 with Explore Worldwide Ltd

It is not intended as a guide since China has changed considerably in the intervening years. Instead, this is a snapshot of the parts of China visited at that particular time and a record of personal experiences in this fascinating country.

This book is dedicated with much love to my husband, David, for his unfailing encouragement and support and for always being there for me.

I would like to thank Explore Worldwide both for providing the holiday and for giving permission for this book to be published. I would also like to thank Yichang China Travel Service for allowing me to reproduce and use the maps from their website, www.chinatourmap.com.

Names have been changed in the interests of privacy.

Chinese Key Periods and Dynasties

Pre-Imperial China

5000 – 1650 BC (approx)	Neolithic Period
1650 – 1027 BC	Shang Dynasty
1027 - 256 BC	Zhou Dynasty

Imperial China

221 – 206 BC	Qin Dynasty
206 BC – 9 AD	Former Han Dynasty
9 – 24 AD	Xin Dynasty
25 – 220 AD	Later Han Dynasty
221 – 265 AD	The Three Kingdoms
265 – 316 AD	Western Jin Dynasty

Middle Empire

The Tartar Partition 317 – 589 AD

386 – 550 AD	Tuoba Wei Dynasty
550 - 577 AD	Northern Qi Dynasty
317 – 420 AD	Eastern Jin
502 – 557 AD	Liang Dynasty
589 - 618 AD	Sui Dynasty
618 – 906 AD	Tang Dynasty
907 – 960 AD	Five Dynasties
960 – 1279 AD	Song Dynasty

Late Empire

1279 – 1368 AD	Yuan Dynasty
1368 - 1644 AD	Ming Dynasty
1644 - 1911 AD	Qing Dynasty

1

Hong Kong

Sunday 10th October

It was after dark and the Wanchai district of Hong Kong Island was illuminated by a dazzling array of vivid neon signs. Many vertical signs displaying Chinese characters had horizontal equivalents in English, promoting places such as the Boston Restaurant, the Pizza Bar Pub and Restaurant and the Neptune Pub and Disco.

Brightly lit double-decker trams, painted with gaudy advertisements for the various attractions of the city, sped up and down the main road, taking priority over the cars.

"Which way would you like to go now?" asked David. He added, "I wouldn't mind taking the Star Ferry across the harbour, to see the lights reflected in the water."

Just at that moment, I saw a sign to the Peak Tram. "Let's go and see what it costs to go up the Peak," I suggested. "If it's too expensive, we can always head for the Star Ferry terminal instead."

It took us about fifteen minutes to reach the entrance to the Peak Tram, a cog railway up the mountain in the centre of Hong Kong Island. The cost of the return trip turned out to be well within our budget and a tram was due to depart shortly so we bought tickets, entered one of the waiting carriages and sat down.

As we left the station, the front of the carriage tilted to an angle of about 45° and because all the seats were fixed in position, facing forwards, we found we were leaning back at right angles to the slope. I looked out of the window and then nudged David.

"Look at the skyscrapers," I said. As we slowly ascended past brightly lit buildings, we had the distinct impression that the skyscrapers were leaning over towards us.

"I saw an advert on the side of one of the trams in town that said 'Hong Kong Leans On The Peak,'' remarked David. "Now I know what it means."

From the terminus at the top of the Peak, we walked to a viewing point and I was delighted by the glowing panorama spread out below us. It was a clear night, we were now nearly eighteen hundred feet above sea level and between the illuminated areas of Hong Kong Island and the mainland, the moving lights of ships and ferries were crossing the dark pool of the harbour.

"I'm so glad we came up here," I said. "It's wonderful."

We were at the start of a long-awaited tour through China. Only three weeks previously, I had been in hospital undergoing tests and wondering whether we would be able to make the trip. Fortunately, after about ten days, I had been released with an almost clean bill of health, my symptoms having been put down to a virus which had left me with nothing worse than a leaking heart valve.

We had flown from Heathrow at ten o'clock British Summer Time the previous morning, landing in Hong Kong twenty four hours later at five o'clock in the afternoon, local time. The journey had been broken up by stopovers in Bahrain, Muscat and Bangkok and at each of these places, we had been allowed off the aircraft to wander around and stretch our legs. In between, we had been well fed and had managed to snatch a little sleep but had still felt exhausted on arrival.

From the airport, we had been taken to the Wanchai district of Hong Kong Island, checking in at the Harbour View Hotel, formerly the YMCA. A hot bath and change of clothing had left us feeling somewhat revived and ready to explore our surroundings.

At the hotel Reception desk, we had changed a small amount of money into Hong Kong dollars. As we were leaving for mainland China at lunchtime the following day, we only needed enough currency for sightseeing that evening and the following morning and to cover the cost of our evening meal and a picnic lunch. Breakfast at the hotel was included.

From Reception, we had also obtained a map showing the location of the hotel, to help us to find our way around.

"I'd like something hot to eat before we do anything else," said David as we left the hotel. We had nearly reached the shopping centre before I saw anywhere selling food.

"Look, there's a Pizza Palace over the road," I said, pointing it out. "Does that appeal to you?"

"I'd rather find somewhere Chinese."

It was David who spotted the Island Hot Pot Restaurant. Through the window, we saw a young Chinese couple sitting at a table, in the centre of which stood a plate piled high with food. Around this bubbled a circular inset pan of boiling water. They were using chopsticks to drop raw food from the centre plate into the water and to transfer cooked food to their bowls.

"That looks interesting," he said. "Let's go in and see what they charge." We went inside and a waiter came over to us.

"Do you have a menu in English?" I asked.

"There is no menu," he replied.

"How much is the Hot Pot?" asked David.

The price was, unfortunately, more than we could afford but the waiter suggested a cheaper alternative of ready-cooked rice, chicken and vegetables and we ordered one helping between us.

While we waited to be served, we went over to the other couple and found that the young man could speak perfect English.

"Hot Pot is a traditional dish from Sichuan," he told us. "The food is sliced very thinly so it cooks in only a few seconds and the water is spiced to give added flavour. You should try it."

"We will," David assured him. "We're about to take a tour through China which includes Sichuan Province, so I'm sure we'll be having the Hot Pot while we're there."

"When do you go?" asked the young man.

"Tomorrow," I replied.

"We've always lived in Hong Kong but we've never been to China," he said, wistfully. "Enjoy your tour."

We thanked the couple and returned to our table for our own meal, which proved to be very tasty and quite sufficient.

We were now at the top of the Peak and I was mesmerised by the view. After we had been there for a few minutes, David saw a sign for the Panorama Walk. We followed it and found a path encircling the summit of the Peak with superb views over the city and harbour, although there were darker areas on the other side.

We stayed up there until ten o'clock and then reluctantly made our way back to the tram. Everyone else had decided to return at the same time so we joined a queue and by the time we were down and had walked back to our hotel, it was about eleven o'clock. We were now exhausted but we had had an excellent first evening.

Monday 11th October

After a good night's sleep, we felt fully restored and we were up at half past six to pack the few items we had needed overnight. At seven o'clock, we went down to breakfast and found that the restaurant offered an international buffet with both Western and Chinese food. At that time of day, we were very happy to choose Western food.

The previous evening, Austin, our tour leader, had asked us to meet up with the group in the lobby after breakfast, so that he could check insurance documents and give us some information about the holiday. Accordingly, when we had eaten, I went to our room to collect our insurance papers, a notebook and a pen and returned to sit with David in the Reception area.

We had already made the acquaintance of some of our group during the flight stopovers and on the drive from the airport. While we waited for Austin, we introduced ourselves to a few more of our fellow travellers.

We were all from Britain apart from John, a tall, lanky Canadian in his sixties, with dark-rimmed glasses and dark receding hair, who had arrived earlier the previous day from Edmonton, Alberta. There were twenty four of us altogether, an unusually large group for an Explore holiday.

At nine o'clock, we were joined by Austin, a stocky young man in his mid-twenties, with a friendly round smiling face and short curly fair hair. Having made sure that we were all present, he took us up the stairs to a first floor conference room, where we all sat around a long table.

After checking that we all had adequate insurance, Austin gave us a short summary of his experience as an Explore tour leader before we each introduced ourselves to the group. Austin then briefly ran through the tour itinerary and explained about FECs, the foreign exchange currency, and renminbi, the currency used by the local people.

"The Chinese currency is the yuan and FECs come in notes worth one hundred, fifty, ten, five and one yuan. There are also FEC notes for one and five jiao. Ten jiao equal one yuan." He walked round the table, holding up samples of FECs so that we would be able to recognise them.

"When you buy anything," he continued, "you will probably be given change in renminbi, which you can spend in the markets or use for small items like drinks, but otherwise you will be expected to pay in FECs. These are renminbi notes." He showed us examples for comparison.

"There are also renminbi coins for one yuan and for jiao and fen. Ten fen equal one jiao." He passed round some of the coins for us to look at.

"The official rate of exchange is one renminbi to one FEC, although you may be offered half as much again on the black market. However, you should refuse any such offer as you're likely to be given old, worthless currency. To be on the safe side, I suggest you purchase all your FECs through me as I have reliable contacts."

At ten o'clock, the briefing was over and we were free until ten minutes to twelve, when we would have to bring our luggage down to Reception, ready for a noon departure.

David and I still had some change left from the previous day so, because the hotel was situated close to the Star Ferry terminal, we decided to walk across and ask the price of a return ticket to Kowloon on the mainland.

"If we need to, we can always come back to the hotel and change a little more money," suggested David.

When we reached the ticket office, the woman in the kiosk asked, "Do you want to travel inside on the lower deck or would you prefer to be on the more expensive upper deck?"

"What would it cost to travel on the upper deck?" enquired David. When he found that the price was the equivalent of ten pence return, he laughed and said,

"We'll treat ourselves. Two return upper deck tickets, please."

As the ferry left Hong Kong Island, the Peak was almost hidden behind the skyscrapers, but as we drew away across the harbour, the mountain appeared to grow in size, the skyscrapers in the foreground gradually shrinking in comparison. Although the sky was hazy, there was enough sun to sparkle off the wavelets and the water looked green in the morning light. It was only a very short crossing and we were soon disembarking on the other side.

Austin had reminded us that morning that we would have to buy lunch before taking the train to Guangzhou in China, so our first stop in Kowloon was at a supermarket. We were very unadventurous and bought rolls, cheese, which was sliced and put into the rolls for us, and bottled water.

We then had about fifteen minutes for a very quick look at the nearby streets, heavily festooned with shop signs and advertisements which were strung across the busy, traffic-packed roads. Chinese characters were displayed horizontally as well as vertically and the signs were so numerous that it was impossible to see very far down the streets. Most signs had an English translation underneath.

"It's time we were getting back," David said anxiously as I turned another corner.

"I just want a quick photograph," I said. Seconds later, we were hurrying to catch the ferry back to Hong Kong Island.

"I hope we're not going to be late," he worried as we went on board.

We were relieved to see another couple on the upper deck that we recognised from the group meeting that morning.

"We thought we might be the last back," said David as we introduced ourselves again. With the number of people in the group, it was impossible to remember everybody's name.

The couple, in their early fifties, were Julie and Chris from Oldham in Lancashire. Chris, who worked for the Inland Revenue, was tall and broad shouldered, his fine fair hair, which was thinning on top, being ruffled by the breeze. Julie, a social worker, was much shorter and very slim, with shoulder length straight dark hair and spectacles.

"Don't worry," said Chris. "It's not far to the hotel and it will take a few minutes to get all the cases loaded into the coach."

From the ferry terminal, we hurried back in the humid midday heat, arriving with five minutes to spare. David and I rushed up to our room and brought down the luggage and, while he took the cases out to the coach, I handed in the key and checked us out. Most of the others were already on the coach when we found our seats.

When we arrived at the railway station in Kowloon, we collected our bags and followed Austin inside.

"Leave the luggage here and you can take it in turns to watch it," he suggested. "I'm going to collect our train tickets which will probably take about half an hour. You can wander round the station forecourt while you're waiting. There are several shops where you can spend any Hong Kong dollars you have left. Please meet me back here at one o'clock."

As we all put our cases down, we noticed that John had a flat bag that looked almost empty.

"You haven't brought much with you," said David candidly.

"He's perfected the art of travelling light," chuckled Mandy, a slim, neat woman in her fifties with very short grey hair that lay close to her head like a cap.

"It's so easy," said John. "I wash things out every night so all I need is a change of underwear and socks, a pullover and a spare shirt. I've been to China before so I know that toiletries are provided in every hotel."

In our bathroom at the Harbour View Hotel, we had noticed a small cellophane-wrapped bar of soap, two combs, two toothbrushes, a small tube of toothpaste and a little bottle of shampoo but it would never have occurred to us to travel without such items in a sponge bag.

Jane and Phil, a couple in their late thirties who ran a hardware business in Stamford, offered to look after the cases while the rest of us wandered off.

David and I only had some small change left and when we had looked at what was for sale, we found we had just enough to buy two bags of sweets. We went back to the luggage to give Jane and Phil a chance to look round and while we were waiting, opened one of the bags.

The sweets inside were wrapped in brightly coloured cellophane with Chinese symbols and pictures of people and flowers. David unwrapped one of the sweets and popped it into his mouth.

"Ugh," he said, grimacing. "It's horrible. It tastes like very salty liquorish."

I tried one with a different wrapping and found that it, too, had the flavour of salty liquorish. I discreetly wrapped it back in its paper and put it in my pocket until I could find a handy litter bin. When the others came back, we disposed of the rest of our sweets by handing them around and in return, were able to try some of their food purchases, which tasted equally outlandish to our Western palates.

Austin returned with the tickets.

"Are we all here?" he asked. We were. "Then follow me."

We took our cases and joined the queue of passengers for the train to China. Because we were leaving what was still, at that time, British territory, we had to pass through Customs and show our passports.

The train was already waiting at the platform and once we had cleared Customs, Austin said, "We're in carriage 8, guys. This way."

We all followed him and when we reached our carriage, Austin climbed on board first to help with lifting the luggage on to the train. The bags were then stored in a compartment at the end of the carriage and locked in for safekeeping. Austin removed and kept the key.

"Sit anywhere you like," he told us. "We have the whole carriage to ourselves." Once we were seated, he handed out the train tickets with the appropriate seat numbers on them.

"Keep these handy in case a ticket inspector comes to check them."

We had been booked into a soft-seat carriage, with blue net curtains up at the windows and matching blue antimacassars over the blue padded seat backs. The seats were in sets of four on either side of the carriage and between each set of seats was a table with a thermos flask of boiling water fastened beneath it and a vase of plastic flowers on top.

"The Chinese have a long-held custom of boiling their drinking water, which has probably saved them from many epidemics in the past," Austin remarked. "It's quite safe to drink. In China, you'll find a thermos flask of freshly boiled water provided in your hotel room every night."

The train left on time at ten past two and we set off at a very sedate pace, the train trundling along at between ten and twenty miles an hour while Chinese music played softly from speakers throughout the carriage. It was very relaxing and as we crawled through the New Territories, we ate our picnic lunches.

To make life easier for us, Explore had arranged for a Group Visa listing all our names. While we were eating, Austin collected our passports and numbered them in biro on the back covers, in the order that our names appeared on the Group Visa.

"When we arrive in Guangzhou and whenever we travel by air," he told us before returning them, "I want you to line up in numerical order to file through Customs, so that they can check your names off quickly against the visa details."

The New Territories looked very rural with lakes and forests. Small villages were surrounded by fields divided into neat rectangles of strip farming. During the journey, Austin told us that we would be arriving in Guangzhou, formerly known as Canton, one of the oldest cities in China, situated in the province of Guangdong.

"Back in the eighteenth and early nineteenth centuries, British traders in Canton had exclusive rights to the Chinese opium trade," he informed us. "The Chinese demand for opium was so high that they were importing up to three hundred thousand pounds in weight of opium every year, which they paid for in tea, silk and silver. This was impoverishing the country so, in an effort to stamp out the opium trade, the Chinese laid siege to the British in Canton in 1839 and cut off their food supplies, until they surrendered their opium stocks."

"The British retaliated by attacking China in what became known as the first Opium War," he continued. "This war lasted for two years until there was a peace treaty, under which Hong Kong Island and part of Kowloon were ceded to the British."

"I wondered how Hong Kong came to be British," I said quietly to David.

At five o'clock, exactly on time, we arrived at our destination.

"All of you get off quickly and leave the luggage," Austin told us. He stayed on the train until last, unlocked the baggage compartment and handed the cases down to Dan and Phil who passed them on to the rest of us. As he brought the last case down and joined us, he declared, "I've found from experience that that's by far the quickest way of getting all the luggage off the train."

At the end of the platform, we all lined up in Group Visa order with our passports at the ready and we were quickly through the checks and entering China.

2

Guangzhou

Guangdong Province

As we left the station, we were met by Vicky, our local guide in Guangzhou, and Li Mei, our national guide who would be with us throughout our time in China.

Vicky was a tiny, very pretty young girl in her late teens or early twenties with dark eyes and shoulder length black wavy hair.

Li Mei, who appeared to be in her late thirties, was of medium height and build with a round face and high cheekbones. She wore her black hair pulled tightly back and twisted into a bun and had a serious expression on her face, which probably made her look older than she actually was.

"We must hurry," Vicky told us as she hustled us out to the coach, which was waiting a few yards away with its engine running. "We go straight to the restaurant for our evening meal because they will not serve after six o'clock."

The driver took our cases and rapidly packed them into the luggage compartments on either side of the coach while we found seats inside. Within minutes, we were on our way.

Being the largest city in southern China, Guangzhou had the usual rush hour traffic problems, compounded by hundreds of cyclists who ignored the rules of the road and were cutting across and against the general traffic flow. Our driver was trying to thread his way through the congestion to get us to the restaurant as quickly as possible when we were shaken by a sudden jolt and the coach came to a standstill.

"What's happened?" asked Phil.

Austin, who was sitting at the front, turned round and told us, "We've just caught the back of a car that seems to have become jammed against the kerb of a roundabout. The paintwork has been scraped and the car looks pretty badly dented."

Vicky was most perturbed and spoke rapidly to our driver, obviously concerned that any delay might result in us missing dinner. Both drivers got out and inspected the damage but, much to Vicky's relief, the car driver was evidently persuaded after a short discussion that the damage was not serious enough to worry about. Our driver climbed back on board and we continued on our way.

We soon arrived at the restaurant, where strings of white fairy lights formed a canopy over the entrance. The interior was hung with tinsel decorations and was deserted, apart from a couple of hovering waiters.

Our group was shown to two large circular tables, each with a spinning Lazy Susan in the centre. As soon as we sat down, one of the waiters took our drinks orders while the other started bringing in a selection of dishes which had obviously been pre-ordered and placed them on the Lazy Susans.

In front of each of us was a small porcelain bowl and a pair of wooden chopsticks wrapped in cellophane, their narrow ends propped up on a carved wooden rest. David and I had already tried using chopsticks in Hong Kong but there we were able to cheat, as Western cutlery was also provided on request. Here, we were not given the option.

Austin was seated at our table and demonstrated the correct way to hold and use the chopsticks and we began to practise. A ceramic serving spoon was provided with the large bowl of rice.

"This is 'sticky rice'," said Austin. "You need to put some of this in the bottom of your bowl and then add to it from the other dishes."

We each helped ourselves to a spoonful or two of rice and found that when we came to eat this with our chopsticks, it could be lifted out in clumps rather than by individual grains, which made life easier.

The other dishes on the Lazy Susan included tofu or bean curd, chopped mild red, yellow and green peppers, green beans and a variety of green leafy plants mixed with nuts. There was also a dish of small bones. Each of these items we had to pluck from the plates with our chopsticks to put into our individual bowls.

After a little practice, I became reasonably adept at this although I found it quite difficult to handle the smooth shiny nuts and the small bones, which had tiny pieces of meat attached. These had to be turned and held firmly to access the meat, which I found much more difficult to accomplish. In the end, I gave up and held them between my fingers.

Most of the dishes, including the bowl of rice, also had minuscule pieces of meat mixed in with them.

"It's fortunate that there are no vegetarians in the group," said Austin, having checked this out earlier. "The Chinese have no concept of vegetarianism and you will usually find some meat incorporated into every dish other than tofu. If you don't eat meat, this makes for a very monotonous diet."

We each had to wait our turn before spinning a particular dish towards us on the Lazy Susan and it then took time to transfer the food to our bowls and from there to our mouths, so it was a slow, leisurely meal. We were quietly chatting to each other or concentrating on trying to eat when, suddenly, Anna screamed and leapt up on to her chair.

She was an attractive girl in her early twenties with long dark hair tied in a pony tail. She had come away with her mother, Anita, who was sitting at the other table, while Anna had teamed up with the younger people in the group, Liz and her friend Jess from London and Mattie who was with her boyfriend, Josh, from Norwich.

Anita jumped out of her seat and rushed over to see what had happened. “What’s the matter?” she cried.

We were all looking at Anna as she raised her leg and shook it in panic. A large rat was dangling from her trousers by its teeth. It let go, dropped to the floor and ran off across the restaurant.

“Are you all right, Anna?” asked Austin, full of concern, as the rest of us peered under the table and chairs looking for any other rats that might be hiding there. Anita put a protective arm round her daughter who had now climbed down from her chair.

“Yes, I’m OK,” Anna answered, a little shaken, as she inspected her leg. “The skin isn’t broken. It’s a good job I’m wearing thick trousers.”

Then she told us, “As I was eating, I felt something touch my leg and when I moved it back, I felt a weight lean against my ankle. That’s when the rat sank its teeth into my trousers.”

There was a short period of mayhem while the kitchen staff chased the rodent and cornered it at the far end of the restaurant. A waiter knocked it unconscious, popped it into a saucepan and carried it through to the kitchen. We realised it must have escaped from there and would probably be served for lunch the following day. We resumed our meal but most of us now had our legs tucked under us on the chairs to be on the safe side.

Looking at the empty plate which had held the small bones and the dishes of vegetables and rice mixed with tiny pieces of meat of unknown origin, David grimaced and said to me, "We've probably been eating rat all this time without knowing it."

"It's a bit late to worry about it now," I said, being practical. "At least it seemed well cooked."

When we had finished our meal and it was time to pay, none of us had any Chinese currency so Austin said, "Don't worry, I'll settle up and we'll sort it out in the morning. If you each let me have £20.00 over breakfast, I'll give you the change in FECs."

From the restaurant, we were taken by coach to our hotel, the Bai Yun or White Cloud, a large modern building more than thirty storeys high that towered over its surroundings. David and I had a room up on the twentieth floor but it was now too dark to see the view.

As soon as we had unpacked what we needed for the night, David and I went for a walk. Nearby, we found a building with the lights on and a sign in English proclaiming that it was a Friendship Store. Although it was nearly nine o'clock, the doors were still open.

"Let's go in and have a look round," I suggested.

Once inside, we appeared to be the only customers and the shop assistants were very friendly and anxious to be of service. They all seemed able to speak English.

"We're just looking to see what you sell," I said to them. "We only arrived in China this evening so we don't want to buy anything yet."

The shop stocked a variety of goods from clothing to furniture, with a large section devoted to tinsel decorations. We were fascinated to find that there was an abacus on each counter, for the employees to calculate the cost of purchases and any change required.

"How does that work?" asked David, pointing to one of these and a young assistant demonstrated, sliding the wooden markers along at amazing speed. Although she tried to explain the system, which she said was simple, we remained mystified.

When we left the Friendship Store, everywhere else looked closed. We returned to the hotel and stood in the lobby chatting to some of the others in our group before retiring to bed.

Tuesday 12th October

The next morning dawned bright and sunny, if a little misty. Looking out of our bedroom window, we saw below us a six-lane highway busy with buses, although there were, surprisingly, no cars or bicycles at that time. The pavements were full of people scurrying to work, looking almost like ants from this height.

On our side of the road, we were looking down on the roofs of concrete blocks of offices or flats, between six and ten storeys high. Directly opposite the hotel on the far side of the road was a small area of parkland, to one side of which stood an office building, ten storeys high, dwarfed by tall concrete skyscrapers towering behind.

The previous evening, Austin had asked us to bring our luggage down to the foyer before breakfast. "It will be collected from there and taken direct to the airport," he had told us. We repacked the items we had used overnight, took the cases down in the lift and left them with the others belonging to our group.

In the dining room, we were relieved to find that, once again, there was the option of Western food. Not fancying the Chinese selection of cabbage soup, rice and vegetables for breakfast, we made our choice from the Western dishes.

During the meal, Austin came round to collect £20.00 from each of us and the equivalent in Canadian dollars from John. He had already calculated how much was due after deducting the cost of the previous evening's meal, so it did not take long to hand out the FECs.

"That should be enough to last you for a few days. You can exchange more tonight if you need it, once I've had a chance to go to the Bank again," he said.

At half past eight, Vicky and Li Mei joined us and we set off in the coach to see the sights. We soon discovered that although Vicky looked very decorative, she was annoyingly giggly, probably due to nerves, and spoke very little English. However, Li Mei and Austin were able to supplement the small amount of information she gave us, so it was not a problem.

"Guangzhou is called the City of Flowers, because it is situated on the Tropic of Cancer and the weather is always warm," Li Mei told us as we were being driven through the city. "Our first visit today will be to the Chen Clan Temple built in 1810, one of the very few temples to survive the Cultural Revolution. At one time, each clan or family had their own temple, on which they would lavish most of their wealth in honour of their ancestors."

"This was a Taoist temple," Austin added. "The family would come here to offer their food to the ancestors, before eating it themselves. The building is now a museum."

The driver parked the coach at the side of the street, only a short walk from the temple, which consisted of separate buildings linked together by narrow entrances. The outer walls of the temple were constructed in a light coloured brick and just below the eaves were panels carved with scenes of ancestral gatherings.

The overhanging roofs were tiled in bamboo, the ends sealed with green disks. From a distance, the wavy surface gave the appearance of corrugated iron. However, it was the decorations on top of the roofs that caught the eye.

Along the top ridge of each roof ran a deep beam carved with brightly painted exotic birds perched on branches bearing blossom and fruit, plus panels of more abstract designs. Above the beam were additional intricate, detailed carvings of varying heights, representing temples and gateways intermixed with dragons and tiny people in different poses, the light showing through in between.

The sides of each roof carried red triangular wedges with designs superimposed in gold and green. The wide end reached to the top of the ridge carvings, narrowing to a point at the lower edge of the roof. These wedges were quite broad, each with its own overhanging bamboo roof and a raised parapet down the centre. On the lower half of this balanced a line of colourful carvings fronted by large-eyed red and gold lions, laughing at each other across their own section of roof and looking as though they had just had fun sliding down the length of the parapet.

Above each entrance archway was a deep façade. This framed a three dimensional image, painted in shades of green, blue, red, white and gold, of a room containing a family in traditional Chinese costume. Centrally above this stood the statue of an ancestor god, robed in red. He was balanced on the head of a dolphin or carp, flanked on either side by another fish, its tail waving high in the air.

We were allowed time to take in all this fabulous detail before going through into a central courtyard, to find a similar family carving over the archway on the other side, with another ancestor standing on the head of the central fish of a set of three.

In the courtyard, the top and sides of each roof were just as beautifully decorated but the roofs extended beyond the buildings and were supported on carved wooden beams and crossbars. These provided an open shaded walkway around the courtyard, giving access to the rooms of the museum.

The first room we entered housed some very large, detailed and delicate three-dimensional ivory carvings of landscapes, where mountains, trees, buildings and bridges all intertwined. There was also a very intricate miniature carving, so tiny that it could only be viewed through a magnifying glass.

A second room contained a collection of inkstones. "What were these used for?" asked David. Li Mei replied.

"The ink came in solid sticks and the ink stones were used to grind them into a powder," she explained. "They were in regular use from the seventh century AD and were often carved with the design of a dragon. Many had a cavity for storing the ink powder, mixed with water. The best inkstones were prized as they made inks of a very fine quality and texture which could be used to produce high grade calligraphy and painting."

Another room had wooden door panels of lacy wooden fretwork which surrounded carvings of, for example, men on horseback or ships at sea. There were also deep blue glass panels set in wooden latticework, with flowers and butterflies etched in white against the blue.

Out in the open courtyard was a wooden stand holding tiers of miniature bonsai trees, each in its own shallow ceramic dish. Across the road from the temple was a school and as we walked around in the warm sunshine, we were accompanied by the sound of children chanting their lessons in chorus. It was delightful.

From the temple, we returned to the coach and as we set off again, Li Mei told us, "We're now going to Yun Xio or Five Rams Park. The Five Rams were gods who brought the first rice grains from heaven and showed the people how to plant them. Because of the climate and fertility of the soil, three rice crops a year can be grown in this area. That's why the city flourished here and the Five Rams are the symbol of Guangzhou."

The park was set on the side of quite a steep hill. The coach stopped at the top of the hill, close to a statue of the five rams standing on a rocky cliff, the largest ram perched on a raised rock in the centre.

Austin took us across to three very large carved stone blocks nearby which illustrated the rice legend. The first stone depicted the descent of the gods and the people accepting the rice seeds, the second showed the planting of rice in the paddy fields and the third pictured the harvest celebrations. In the centre of the latter, flanked by a banana palm and a laden fruit tree, two dancing men carried a huge stook of rice. On their right were women bearing large baskets of fruit and vegetables while on their left were musicians playing traditional instruments for a line of dancing women.

From here, we wandered down the hill towards a lake with a wooded island in the centre. Austin and Li Mei were taking their time and we stopped to watch a tai chi instructor with a group of elderly pupils. The tai chi movements were slow and graceful and required a good sense of balance.

"The Chinese are very keen on exercise and can be found practising tai chi in secluded places at any time of day, although first thing in the morning before work is the most popular time," remarked Austin.

"Do you think they'd mind if we joined in?" David asked Li Mei.

"I'm sure that would be all right," she said, so David and I, followed by Anita and Anna, walked round towards the back of the class. Anita, in her fifties with short, blonde, curly hair, was a yoga teacher so, unlike us, she was very fit and supple.

We were welcomed with beaming smiles and did our best to copy the movements for a few minutes while the Chinese were clearly amused by our efforts. Some of the others in our group looked disapproving but we were enjoying ourselves and ignored them.

John walked over to Austin. "I don't want to complain," he said. "The park is very pleasant but there must be more interesting places to see."

"To tell you the truth," Austin confessed, "I negotiated a visit here as an alternative to the Sun Yat Sen Memorial, at the request of earlier groups."

After leaving the park, we were taken to a porcelain factory. We watched the women painting dishes and bowls before going through to the shop. Because all the china was hand-painted, the items were very expensive and none of us was tempted to buy. As we stood around, Joanne and Gordon, a couple in their mid forties from Edinburgh, grumbled firstly to each other and then to Austin.

"We feel we're wasting time again," Gordon complained. "Surely there are other sights you could take us to."

"I'm sorry," said Austin, "but I was unable to negotiate any alternative to the factory visit." He then explained to us all.

"Each local guide is required to take every tour group round at least one factory and the guide receives commission on everything sold to the group. One of my first groups dug their heels in after a few such visits and when they arrived at yet another factory, they refused to leave the coach. The local guide burst into tears and ran away and we never saw her again. I later found out that if a tour group fails to visit a factory, the guide is fined according to the number of people in the group. As a guide isn't well paid, this is a serious problem."

Now that we understood the reason, we were prepared to accept the factory visits but hoped to keep them as brief as possible. We had to stay for fifteen minutes before returning to the coach.

After we set off again, Li Mei told us, "We're now on our way to Ching Ping market."

Chen Clan Temple

Ching Ping Market

She added, "I think you'll find it interesting. The Cantonese have a reputation for eating anything that moves."

Ching Ping Market spread out into narrow streets with overhanging roofs and was quite an eye-opener. To ensure that meat was fresh, much of it was sold live. Tiny cages and wicker baskets were crammed with dogs, cats, birds, rabbits, mice, rats and squirrels, while maggots, terrapins, crabs, eels and snakes were kept in bowls. Some of the reptiles, barely covered with water, were being turned regularly by hand to keep them alive.

"Look up there," said David. "Aren't those dogs?" The animals appeared to have been stripped of their fur and roasted whole, before being hung from the rafters.

Some stalls were displaying rows of pigs' trotters and birds' heads and claws, plus piles of fat and offal. There were also stalls of vegetables and various types of fungi. However, many of the vendors did not have stalls for their livestock or crops and were selling these from baskets on the ground while they stood or squatted behind them. The smells were strong but varied.

As we walked around, we flinched at the sound of some of the men very noisily clearing their throats of phlegm, which they then spat out into the gutter. It was quite nauseating, so we made a joke about it adding to the flavour of the food and giving marks out of ten for the dreadful gargling noise. Lunch was laid on in a restaurant next to the market but by then, most of us had lost our appetites.

After lunch, we were driven back across the city. We went over a bridge and Austin told us, "We're now crossing the Pearl River." This seemed somewhat of a misnomer since the water below us was a thick viscous-looking green-brown with a white scum floating on top.

Further on, we came to a roundabout where a man was sweeping the road very, very slowly.

"I'm sure we passed that same man sweeping round the same roundabout hours ago, when we were on our way to the Chen Clan Temple," laughed Chris.

"It's quite likely," said Austin. "The Chinese Government guarantees everyone a job so there's no particular incentive to work hard."

When we reached Guangzhou airport, we said goodbye to Vicky and Austin took us to the left luggage office where the hotel staff had delivered our cases that morning. The porter behind the desk brought out from a back room all the cases bearing an Explore label.

"Each of you will need to identify your own bag," said Austin, indicating his own which was passed over the counter.

Once we all had our cases, we handed them back at the check-in desk, from where they were wheeled out on trolleys to load into the hold of the waiting China Southern aeroplane. Having had our tickets and visa checked, we then strolled from the terminal building across the tarmac to the sleek modern aircraft and boarded, ready for the three o'clock flight to Guilin.

3

Guilin

Guangxi Province

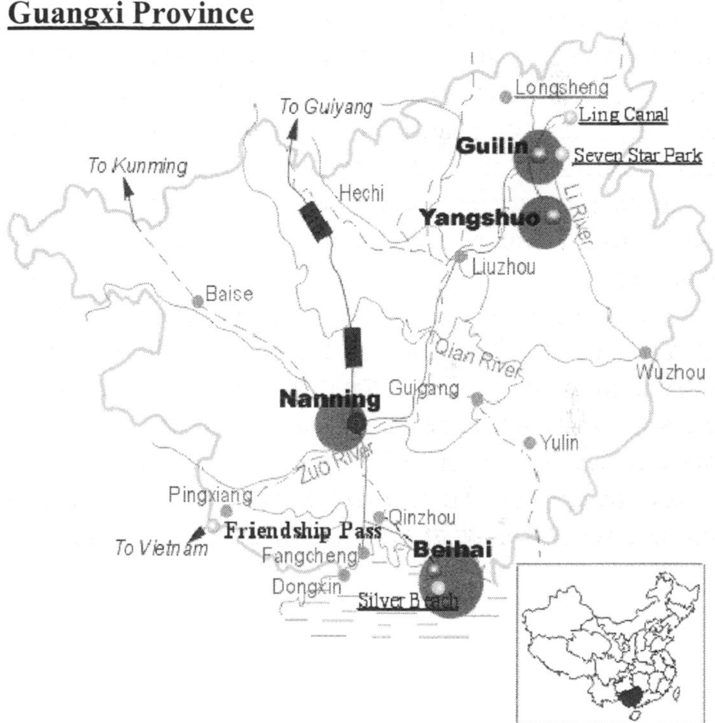

During the flight, we were served with drinks and packets of peanuts. We arrived in Guilin at a quarter past five and once we had collected our luggage and made our way to the exit, we met our new local guide, a small dark man in his late twenties with a bright intelligent face. He greeted us with a smile and introduced himself.

"My name is Long, meaning 'Dragon'," he said. "Welcome to Guilin. Please, follow me to the coach."

As we made our way to the hotel, Long told us that Guilin means 'Forest of Acacia Trees'. Our hotel was very modern and luxurious, situated across the road from a lake.

Austin obtained the keys and list of room numbers from Reception and as he handed out the keys, he said, "Just take your luggage up to your rooms and come straight down again. We must be in the hotel restaurant in the next few minutes, so they can finish serving us before six o'clock. We'll then be going on a river trip so bring down whatever you're likely to need and make sure you have plenty of insect repellent with you."

After an excellent meal, we set off in the coach on the short journey to the Li River and on the way, David and I liberally covered all our exposed skin in strong smelling insect repellent.

As we arrived, Long said, "We're going to take a boat out on the river to watch the cormorant fishermen at work. Please keep together and follow me."

He led us to a small pleasure cruiser moored nearby. It was very dark, clouds blotting out any light from the moon and stars, but the dim glow from a few lanterns enabled us to board and climb to the upper deck. The air above the river was thick with mosquitoes.

As I opened my mouth to say something to David, several flew inside. I coughed, spluttered and spat them out and then kept my mouth tightly closed for the rest of the evening to avoid swallowing any.

The cruiser took us to the centre of the river and we leaned over the deck railing and gazed down on the fishermen below. They were sitting on long narrow rafts with a lamp shining at either end. Each fisherman crouched in the stern in front of a large wicker basket and steered with a paddle, while several cormorants stood along the centre of the raft.

These birds took it in turns to dive into the river, each returning a few moments later with the tail of a fish hanging from its beak. Its owner held the cormorant upside-down by its legs over the basket at the back of the raft until the fish dropped out. The bird was then placed back on the raft until it was ready to dive again.

"The fishermen breed from their own cormorants, which lay up to five eggs a year," Long informed us as we watched, fascinated. "They start training the birds early by tying the necks of the young hatchlings, so they can only swallow the smallest fish. The birds are starved during the day and at night, they swim for the fish which are attracted by the lights on the raft. Cormorants are expert hunters and when one catches a large fish, its head sticks in the bird's throat, leaving its tail hanging out. The cormorant is trained to return to the raft where the fish is added to the catch in the basket and the cormorant goes diving for another fish. From time to time, the cormorants are rewarded with titbits of smaller fish which they can swallow."

While the process was being explained to us, the baskets on the rafts were being filled rapidly. It seemed a very effective, if perhaps slightly cruel method of fishing.

Long and the fishermen seemed not to notice the mosquitoes and we wondered whether they had built up some sort of immunity over the years. It had been a fascinating evening but we were glad once we were back inside the hotel.

Wednesday 13th October

When we went down to breakfast, we learned that Austin had received bad news for some of our group. Jenny's mother had died and Dan's father was seriously ill in hospital.

Jenny and her husband Martin were in their fifties, from Solihull. Jenny was a teacher, tall and slim with shoulder-length dark hair in a page-boy cut. Martin, an architect, was also tall, with receding dark hair flecked with grey. They were seated at our table and as we were eating, Jenny told us that her mother had been ill for some years with Alzheimer's.

"Please don't get me wrong," she told us, "but she was in a nursing home and has been unable to recognise Martin and me for some time. I said goodbye to my mother a long while ago. My sister is at home to take care of the funeral arrangements and to be honest, my mother's death has come as somewhat of a relief."

While Jenny and Martin would be continuing with their holiday, Dan and his wife Laura, who were in their late forties and from Beaconsfield, had decided that they would have to return to England as soon as possible. They had asked Austin to arrange return flights for them and were leaving that evening. (Many years later, we met Dan on another Explore trip and he told us how thankful they were that they went back when they did, as they had been able to speak to his father for one last time before he passed away.)

This would be the last day of their holiday and it was certainly a day to remember. We took a four hour cruise along the Li River which flowed between the lovely limestone hills for which this part of China is renowned.

The hills were not high but were precipitously steep. Many were riddled with caves or had sheer cliffs plunging down to the river. The limestone had been uplifted from the seabed about three hundred million years ago, before being eroded into this spectacular and unique landscape which has inspired Chinese artists for many centuries.

When we reached the jetty early that morning, several cruise ships were lined up side by side, some with people already on board. Austin took us to one that had been reserved for our party.

As we went up the gangplank, we were directed into the restaurant below deck and invited to sit on folding wooden seats round long wooden tables, on each of which stood the obligatory vase of artificial flowers. We were then served with beer, soft drinks and packets of salted peanuts.

As we left the shore and the scenery started to slip past, I said to David, "I hope we don't have to spend the whole time down here."

Austin heard me and smiled. "Now that we're under way, you'll be allowed up on deck," he said, adding, "If you're going to spend some time up there, I suggest you take your chairs with you as there's very little seating."

We all folded up our seats and carried them to the upper deck. Luckily there was a handrail to help us to balance as we climbed up the metal ladder. We then discovered that our ship was the fourth in a convoy of five. The day was hot and sunny and we were glad to have a canopy to provide some shade.

We passed a herd of water buffalo standing in the river and although some of them were twenty or thirty yards from the shore, the water did not even reach to the top of the animals' legs. Luckily, we were in a deeper channel, gouged from the centre of the riverbed. Further on, we passed two dredgers, each with rather ramshackle living accommodation attached.

The river then became even more shallow on either side of our channel, broken up by islands of shingle on which grass and wild flowers were beginning to take root. In places, this shingle had completely enclosed part of the river to form a lake, where birds were nesting on green patches of floating weed.

Later, the river narrowed and deepened and we passed under the shadow of the cliffs. Although the steepest rock was exposed, most of the hills were covered in a mantle of vegetation while forests of palm trees and bamboos lined the shore. The bamboo was tall, lush, graceful and verdant and in places, the banks resembled a jungle.

Mandy, the artist in our group, was in her element and rapidly produced several sketches of the wonderful scenery.

"I wish I had your talent," I said to her. "I would love to be able to draw but I haven't the eye for it. I'm better with a camera."

"I'm only putting in the outlines now," she said. "I'll fill in the details later when I have more time." Even with the outline sketches, she had completely captured the atmosphere of the place.

The morning passed quickly and at midday, Austin came round and asked us to return to the restaurant, with our chairs, to have lunch. This was cooked in two woks at the stern of the vessel.

The food was very tasty and included what we had assumed to be seaweed soup when we had eaten it at the restaurant the previous evening. However, that morning, we had passed rafts piled high with river weed and we now decided that this was probably the main ingredient of the soup.

After we had eaten, we carried our chairs back to the upper deck and continued to admire the wonderful scenery. David walked to the stern of the boat and was leaning over the railing when he called to me, "Darling, come and look at this."

I joined him and saw below us two women kneeling on an open projection at the back of the steamer, washing the dirty lunch bowls in the river. It was rather disconcerting. Luckily, unlike the Pearl River, the water in the Li River was beautifully clear and none of us suffered any ill effects from the meal.

The trip was idyllic and very relaxing and all too soon, we reached the town of Yangshuo, eighty kilometres to the south of Guilin. Here the steamers turned at an elegant two span bridge, ready for the return journey.

We disembarked and as we left the ship, each passenger was handed a gift of a small cotton handkerchief printed with the route of the Li River cruise.

As soon as we were all ashore, Austin said, "Quickly now, come with me, keep together and don't stop to look at the stalls." He then hurried us to where our coach was waiting.

We passed dozens of stall holders trying to attract the cruise passengers with T-shirts, scarves, fans and paintings, but there was no time to really see what was available. I then noticed an old man with a straw coolie hat, white wispy beard and long straggly moustache, sitting on a low stool and holding a bamboo pole with a cormorant balanced on each end.

I took a quick snap as I hurried past and there was immediate uproar as the man and his friends demanded payment, which held us up for a few seconds. I had no change, only FECs, but Austin, looking rather annoyed, came to my rescue with a few renminbi.

I was embarrassed that I had delayed everyone and vexed that I had been unable to compose the picture, which had been spoilt by all the people standing around the old man, but there was no time to argue.

The coach driver had his engine running and the moment we were all on board, he tried to leave. However, if the aim of all our hurrying had been to miss the traffic jams, we had failed as the coach remained in the same place for the next twenty minutes.

The driver eventually lost patience and squeezed his way past several other stationary coaches, causing consternation amongst the stall holders and nearly demolishing several of the stalls in the process.

Once we were clear of the port area and travelling through a wide valley, Austin said, "Most coaches stop on the way back to Guilin to allow the passengers to take a photograph of the paddy fields. However, I've persuaded Long that we want to see much more of the countryside than that." Shortly afterwards, our coach left the main road and took a narrow side road to one of the villages.

On the way, Austin informed us, "The farms around here were once all owned by co-operatives and the workers were very poor. They began to leave the farms, crowding into the cities to look for work, particularly during the winter months, leaving the land untended. Now, each family owns its own portion of land, which gives them an incentive to work harder. They have to give the Government fifty per cent of all the crops they grow, with a minimum quota to ensure that the land is utilised, but any spare crops can be sold on the open market. As a result, the farm workers are gradually becoming more prosperous."

Li Mei then stood up and took the microphone. "You may meet some of the local people as we go round a village and they will be very happy if you make the effort to say a word or two of Chinese to them," she said. "I would like you all to learn three phrases. Hello is 'ni hau'. Please repeat after me, 'ni hau'." We dutifully repeated the words several times until she was satisfied.

"Good," she said. "The next phrase I would like you to learn is 'xie xie' meaning 'thank you'." We repeated the words and I wrote them phonetically in my notebook as 'neehow' and 'sheshay'.

Li Mei then taught us the phrase for goodbye, 'zai jian', which I wrote in my notebook as 'tsy chienne'.

Again we repeated the words out loud until she was satisfied.

When we reached the village, the coach was parked and we wandered down the street until we came to a track across the fields which we followed. We were in the centre of a small, completely flat valley surrounded by the limestone hills which rose suddenly, almost vertically, and were thickly wooded.

We crossed a large paddy field, the heads of the ripening green rice plants turning gold in the afternoon sun. Around the edge of the field at the foot of the wooded hills were one and two-storey houses painted white, with roofs that appeared from a distance to be tiled but were probably made from bamboo.

We were passed in the opposite direction by a single man leading his water buffalo on the end of a rope. He carefully kept his gaze averted, so we did not attempt to greet him.

Beyond the paddy field, a variety of crops was being grown on individual allotments, crossed by a line of electricity pylons. This part of the valley was divided into neat rectangular patches, each with its own individual vegetable or salad crop.

"All the plants look very healthy," commented Phil.

"Yes," Austin agreed. "The Chinese believe in replenishing the soil by rotating crops and using animal manure."

A woman wearing a high-crowned straw hat was crouched barefoot beside a pool of muddy water, washing the soil off some spring onions. These she placed in batches on a flat tray-shaped basket, with a very tall curved bamboo handle attached to all four corners.

Li River cruise

Watering the crops

Child care

Guilin village

The woman was barefoot, with her trousers rolled above her knees to protect them from the wet mud. She was concentrating on her work and did not look up as we walked past.

We crossed to a gravel path running along one side of the fields and a young lady came towards us carrying two buckets of water hung from either end of a bamboo pole which she balanced over one shoulder.

"The crops are watered regularly but water must sometimes be carried long distances," Austin pointed out.

As we passed her, we all tried out our first Chinese greeting, "ni hau." The young woman smiled at us and she and Long exchanged a few words.

Soon afterwards, we reached the hills and we climbed a short way before dropping down on the other side into a valley filled with orchards. From the branches above us hung large yellow-green pear-shaped citrus fruits.

"These are tree grapefruit," Austin informed us. "I've tried several and found them rather dry and pithy. Each fruit weighs about a pound so make sure you don't accidentally walk into one."

We ducked under the lower branches which overhung the path, pulled down by the weight of the fruit.

The path brought us to an isolated village which looked very poor, with holes in some of the house walls where the brickwork had crumbled away. The bricks were unevenly laid, giving the impression that each family had built their own house. Washing had been strung up along some of the walls to dry and the street had a few uneven cobblestones laid on the bare earth.

While we waited, Li Mei and Long talked to some of the local people and then came back and told us that they were happy for us to walk around and take photographs. We stayed together as a group and were delighted when one woman invited us into her home.

The double wooden entrance doors bore two poster-sized sheets of paper, each with an orange background colour, printed with what at first appeared to be mirror images of a bearded figure flamboyantly dressed in long green robes, bearing a wicked-looking knife on a long pole. A closer look revealed subtle differences between the two images. A smaller picture with a similar design hung from the centre of the porch roof.

"Those are the guardian gods protecting the house," Austin told us.

Passing through the doors, we entered a large room with sweetcorn and peppers hanging on the walls and grain spread across the earthen floor to dry. There were two wooden benches facing each other and the woman picked up a twig besom, swept the grain into a pile on one side and invited us to sit down. There was only space for eight of us so the rest stood and looked around.

The house was supplied with electricity and a single bare light bulb hung on its cord from the ceiling. A bed was folded against one wall and, rather incongruously, a television set stood on a table near the wooden benches. There was no other furniture.

The woman was very hospitable and offered us tea or coffee, which we declined. She then handed round hazel nuts and segments of tree grapefruit which we felt obliged to accept, so we were able to practise our second Chinese phrase, 'xie xie'. The grapefruit segments were on the dry side but the fruit was quite sweet and I enjoyed my snack.

We were then shown the second room of the house. This was much smaller and was used for storage and cooking, the stove consisting of dry twigs in an old oil drum. There were some printed papers on the wall which the woman proudly pointed out to us.

"She is telling us that these are the school reports of her two children," Li Mei explained.

"I thought there was a one child policy in China," said Anita.

"It's true that most Chinese couples are only allowed one child, but in the country, if the first child is a daughter, they are allowed a second child," said Li Mei. "One woman in this particular village has had three children and was heavily fined as a result."

As we left, we bowed to the woman and thanked her again for her hospitality. "Xie xie, xie xie. Zai jian."

As we explored further, we saw hens foraging in the streets and water running in drainage ditches beside some of the houses. Despite the slightly ramshackle appearance, everywhere looked clean and tidy and it was clear that the locals took a pride in their village.

Most of the houses had images of guardian gods on their doors, some standing, others on horseback and armed with different weapons. Other houses had doors missing or partially covered with makeshift pieces of timber. While most people had washing hung on ropes against the wall to dry, one couple had hung their clothes over horizontal bamboo poles supported on crossed end-poles of bamboo.

Several toddlers were being carried round the village by elderly people, probably their grandparents. One child sat in a baby seat fastened in front of the adult seat on a specially adapted bicycle. As we were watching one old lady putting a small girl down at the side of the street to empty her bladder, Austin told us that babies and toddlers all wore split pants with an opening between the legs.

"These are very practical in a farming community," he said. "There's no need to worry about dirty nappies, which would be a problem when all the water has to be drawn from a well or a village pond."

We had now reached the pond belonging to this particular village. It lay in a hollow at the bottom of a flight of stone steps and we watched as the young woman we had met on the footpath earlier went down the steps to fill her two wooden buckets. She then climbed back up the steps, the weight of the heavy buckets of water bending the pole balanced across her shoulders.

I wondered how many times she had to make the trip from the pond through the orchards, over the low hill and across the fields to water her crops. The water was a muddy yellow with a dozen ducks swimming on it and I hoped that the villagers had another source for drinking and cooking.

"Can we stop here for a moment while I make a quick sketch?" asked Mandy.

"No problem," said Austin.

Mandy sat on the grassy bank above the pond, took crayons and a pad of paper out of her bag and began to draw. A small crowd of villagers quickly gathered round to see what she was doing. They were very friendly and all wanted to look at Mandy's sketch, which was very good. We found that they were as interested in us as we were in them.

Eventually it was time to take our leave and walk back across the fields to where our coach was waiting. The villagers all seemed sorry to see us go and waved to us as we called out our 'zai jians'.

On the outskirts of the village, we passed a wide square of concrete on which various crops had been laid out to dry, with stooks of rice propped up at one end, awaiting threshing.

We saw more water buffaloes with their owners as we walked back across the paddy fields. The scenery was beautiful in the soft evening light with the sun casting long shadows, the colours taking on a warmer hue and the more distant hills vanishing in a hazy mist.

Not long afterwards, as we were travelling back on the coach, darkness fell suddenly. We were taken to our hotel in Guilin and on arrival, hurried straight into the restaurant, just in time to be served before six o'clock. Among the dishes was a plate piled high with what we were now convinced was river weed.

After the meal, we all exchanged addresses with Dan and Laura, promising to stay in touch and wishing them a safe journey as they left by taxi on their way to the airport.

Thursday 14th October

When we awoke the next morning, it was raining but this was not a problem as our first visit after breakfast was to the Reed Flute Cavern.

It was only a short distance from Guilin and as we went there in the coach, Austin told us, "At one time, reeds grew near the mouth of the cave. They were used to make wind instruments and this was how the Reed Flute Cavern got its name."

On arrival, we queued up and were allowed in as a single group with an English-speaking guide. As we entered the cave, Mattie laughed. She was an attractive young art student aged about twenty with waist-length straight blonde hair.

"Hey," she chortled. "Welcome to Santa's Grotto."

Unlike the natural-looking limestone caves we had visited in other countries, the stalactites and stalagmites here were floodlit in vivid reds, yellows, greens and blues.

Visitors entered in groups, each group having its own guide, and as we penetrated further into the caverns, each section was illuminated just long enough for the guide to point out the highlights. As soon as the lights went off, the group was meant to hurry to the next floodlit area.

Some of us dawdled, chatting, and the guide for the following group took out his loud hailer and shouted at us. Julie giggled.

"I think he's asking us to move along," she said. "We'd better catch up with the others."

We learned that one huge cavern had been used as a wartime air-raid shelter and could hold more than a thousand people. As we went through the caves, we were told stories about what the various formations were supposed to represent. While limestone waterfalls were easy to see, other formations were more difficult to visualise. One was said to be a poet who was so mesmerised by the beauty of the caverns that, while he was still pondering on how his words could do it justice, he turned to stone.

Professional photographers with floodlights waited at strategic points throughout the caves, ready to take souvenir portraits of Chinese visitors. We discovered later that such photographers were to be found at all the main tourist sites and often provided robes and fancy hats so that their clients could dress up to have their pictures taken.

As we came out of the caves into the souvenir shop, tea was served in small porcelain cups.

We were allowed fifteen minutes to drink our tea and make our purchases and then it was time to leave in the coach for the compulsory factory visit, this time to a jewellery factory. Here we were able to watch the tiniest of gems being inserted into intricate settings on rings, brooches, necklaces and earrings. We were then served coffee and given time to choose what we wanted to buy. Again, the factory shop was ridiculously expensive. When we left, we were driven to Fopo Hill.

"It's still raining. You'll need your waterproofs," Austin called out cheerfully before we got off the coach. "We're going to climb to the top."

Fopo Hill was only about one hundred and sixty feet high but there were three hundred and twenty five steps winding their way up to the top. We found it quite tiring to climb.

From the summit, we should have had clear views across to Guilin City but by this time, the rain was torrential and all we could see was the Li River below and the looming grey outlines of the hills on the opposite bank. We did not stop long and returned, rather wet, to the coach. As we drove back to Guilin, Austin told us that hidden beneath Fopo Hill was the Cave of the Returned Pearl.

"A child found a pearl in the cave and took it home," he told us, "but he was warned that the pearl belonged to a dragon who would devastate the city if he found his precious jewel missing. The child ran back to the cave and returned the pearl in the nick of time."

We had lunch at the Ronghu Hotel in Guilin. This must have been popular with more affluent visitors because, for the first time, we had to run the gauntlet of beggars, both going into the restaurant and returning to the coach afterwards.

On the way back to our hotel, Austin told us, "You are free for the rest of the afternoon but I'd like you to meet me in Reception at five o'clock to go for the evening meal."

"Have you any recommendations for this afternoon?" asked Phil.

"Some of you may like to cycle into town," Austin suggested. "It's not very far, just across the bridge, on the other side of the lake. Bicycles can be hired from the hotel Reception Desk and are not expensive although they tend to be very basic."

He then added, "By the way, I found out at lunchtime that there will be a display of folk dancing at one of the other hotels this evening and that tickets are still available. Before you go off for the afternoon, I need to know how many of you would be interested, as I have to make the bookings and arrange transport."

When he told us the price, David said, "That sounds reasonable. Would you like to go?"

"It should be fun," I said. "Let's book."

We were surprised to find that only six of us wanted to see the show, David and I, Martin and Jenny and Harry and Lucille, the veterans of the group. Harry was in his early eighties while Lucille, his wife, was in her mid-seventies.

By the time we arrived at our hotel, we had nearly dried out and the rain had stopped, although the clouds still hung low over the hills. Nearly all our friends queued at Reception to hire bicycles but David and I decided to walk into Guilin as the bridge was only a few minutes away.

Austin had provided each of us with a map which showed that most of Guilin was situated between the Li River on one side and a string of lakes on the other. The main street, Zhongshan Lu, ran roughly parallel to and halfway between these.

When we set off round the lake in front of the hotel, we could see the grey, misty outlines of the limestone hills in the distance. As we crossed the bridge, there were very few pedestrians but dozens of cyclists, travelling in both directions, many still wearing their plastic rain capes.

At the far end of the bridge, we were greeted by several people waiting for tourists and offering renminbi in exchange for FECs. We politely declined their offers.

We walked towards the centre of Guilin and found that it was more like a small market town than a city. There were farmers everywhere, bringing in their produce to sell. A common form of transport was the tri-cart, with the front part of a bicycle attached to a square open container between the two back wheels. While some of the containers held vegetables, the majority were carrying livestock, mainly ducks and other poultry.

As we crossed the roads, we soon discovered that although motor vehicles stopped at red traffic lights, the cyclists all ignored them. There were a few pedestrian crossings but all traffic ignored these. Following the example of the locals, we learnt to walk slowly and steadily across the roads while the traffic swerved around us. It was rather unnerving.

The farmers were all selling their wares along the kerbsides in the side streets of Guilin. A few had set out their produce on stalls, with a makeshift covering to keep off the rain, but the majority arranged their fruit and vegetables on pieces of cloth at the side of the road or kept them in the baskets in which they had carried them from the fields.

All the main shops and department stores were situated on Zhongshan Lu, which had a wide central road for motor vehicles. On either side was a row of trees and then another wide lane for bicycles, with occasional cycle parking areas. Flanking these were broad pedestrian walkways, paved in a light grey stone.

As we went round the department stores, we found that, like the local Friendship Store in Guangzhou, every counter had an abacus, even the one selling electronic pocket calculators. In the kitchen departments, we found that pastel colours were evidently in fashion with pale green washing machines, primrose yellow refrigerators and pale pink irons.

Further down the street, I saw a shop selling wrapping paper, cards and paper flowers.

"Let's have a look inside," I suggested.

David followed me in and I went over to the shelves of cards. Here, I picked out one with a cut-out section showing a vase of flowers. Beneath this, it said 'Happy Birthday' in English. I opened it and laughed.

"This looks like a useful, multi-purpose card," I grinned, showing it to David. Inside, below the picture of the vase of flowers, were rows of Santa Clauses and Christmas trees.

We enjoyed our afternoon on our own but all too soon, it was time to return to the hotel to shower and change before meeting the group for the evening meal, which was taken in another building belonging to our hotel.

After the meal, the six of us who had booked for the folk dancing were taken by coach to the Gui Shan Hotel, on the far side of Guilin across the Li River. This hotel had its own theatre and we managed to get seats not far from the stage. We were set for a wonderful evening's entertainment.

Although the dancers were amateurs, they were all full of enthusiasm and gave the impression of thoroughly enjoying themselves, while putting on a very professional performance. They demonstrated dances from all areas of China with beautiful, very colourful costumes and headdresses which were changed for each dance.

Some of these dances were very energetic and involved the men leaping high into the air and turning somersaults; a few consisted of the dancers weaving in and out, making patterns which would have been seen better from above; while others were very slow and graceful, such as the fingernail dance, where the women wore elegant robes and false fingernails about eight inches long.

In between the dances, we were entertained by a singer and an excellent percussion band playing traditional instruments. We were also very impressed by an acrobat who, while balanced upside down on one hand, jumped himself up a flight of steps, on to a stool on top of the steps and then up a pile of wooden blocks which were added, one by one, on top of the stool. He then brushed away the blocks and landed back on the stool, still balancing on that one hand.

There was a great deal of audience participation in the show, with the performers throwing balls into the crowd between dances. Those that caught the balls were either given a small gift or were invited up on stage to learn a dance or to make a short speech.

Towards the end, the lights were dimmed for a slow, graceful candle dance, each of the female dancers having three candles in pink lily-shaped holders, one balanced on her head and one in each hand.

The show ended with the percussion band on stage playing the music for a very fast line dance in which members of the audience were encouraged to participate. David was one of the first to be dragged up on stage. The performance lasted exactly seventy five minutes which we were later told was the standard length of time for any entertainment in China.

On the way back to the hotel, the six of us felt quite exhilarated and sorry that the rest of our group had missed the experience.

4

Kunming

Yunnan Province

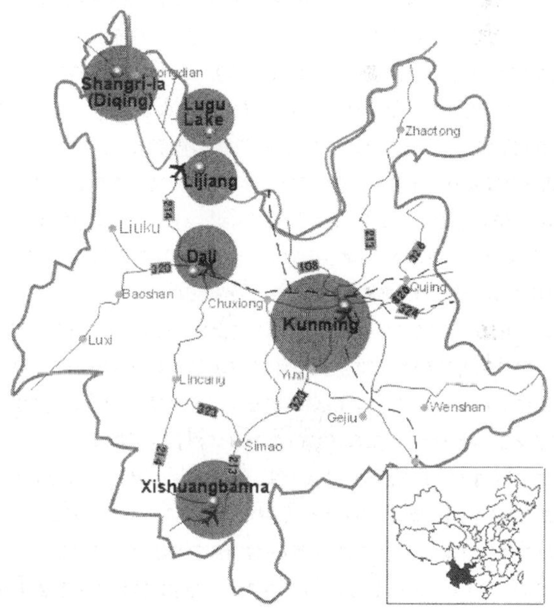

Friday 15th October

The next morning, we were up at five o'clock and having breakfast half an hour later. By a quarter past six, our luggage had been packed on to the coach and we were on our way to the airport.

As we walked across the tarmac to our aircraft, we could see the misty outlines of the limestone peaks stretching out, one behind another, for as far as the eye could see. It was a beautiful area and we were sorry to be moving on but also looking forward to our next destination.

Leaving Guangxi, we headed west to Yunnan, the sixth largest province in China and home to a third of all China's ethnic minority tribes. We landed in Kunming where we would be spending the next three nights. As Austin took us to our coach, it was pouring with rain but still warm.

"Kunming is known as Spring City because of its mild climate," Austin told us, as we made our way to the Jinli Hotel in the city centre.

Once Austin had sorted out our room keys with Reception, we had half an hour to take our luggage to our rooms and freshen up, before returning to the lobby where Austin was chatting to our new local guide. He was in his early thirties, six feet tall and broad shouldered, unlike most of the Han Chinese who tended to be small and slight in build. He introduced himself with a wide grin,

"My name is Lenny – after the Lion."

Lenny turned out to be our favourite local guide. He was friendly and open and spoke excellent English.

"I belong to the Yi tribe, one of at least twenty four minority tribes found in this province," he told us. "I live here in Kunming which is a modern city. Most of the old buildings have been destroyed and replaced with wide streets and modern hotels, offices and apartment blocks. However, this morning, I am going to take you to see what remains of the oldest and most interesting part of Kunming, which includes the market."

We set off on foot in the rain. We passed through an area of tall, functional concrete buildings, but the environment had been made attractive with gardens and the hard outlines of the buildings were softened by trees, lawns and flower beds.

After about ten minutes walking, we came to a street of two storey buildings across which hung numerous banners and rows of brightly coloured bunting. Lenny stopped here.

"This is the beginning of the old city," he told us. "In front of you is the famous 'Yunnan Noodles Across The Bridge Road'." This name meant nothing to David and me but some of the others in the group had obviously heard about it.

Lenny smiled. "I'll tell you a story," he said. "Yunnan's best known dish is a bowl of stewed chicken or duck soup with a thin layer of oil floating on top. It is served with a plate of thin slivers of raw meat, vegetables and rice noodles which are all put into the bowl of soup to cook."

"The story goes," he went on, "that, every day, a woman had to take her husband's lunch across a long wooden bridge to an island in the centre of a lake, where he was studying in isolation for some important examinations. By the time she reached him, the food was always cold. However, one day when she had stewed a fatty chicken, she found that the grease on top of the soup kept it hot. She later discovered that if she added noodles to the soup, they cooked as she crossed the bridge, hence the name of the street."

Lenny led us through the old town, along streets of picturesque, two-storey wooden houses with shops on the ground floor and living accommodation above, dwarfed by the tall modern concrete structures behind them.

We then came to an area with buildings of a similar design but where the wooden facades had been replaced by concrete and the ground floor shops were set back in an arcade, in a compromise between old and new. As we walked around, Lenny decided to tell us more about the Government's single child policy.

"A couple wanting a child requires three separate permits," he began. "To obtain the initial Government permit, the couple must first be accepted on and then complete a training course. Once they have this permit, they must acquire a second permit from the Social Security Office, by proving that they can afford to keep a child. The third permit is the most difficult to obtain and comes from the husband's employer. Each employer is allowed a limited quota of employees, perhaps three a year, who may have a child and permission is given as a reward to the best workers who are otherwise eligible."

Phil laughed. "That gives a whole new meaning to the term 'productivity bonus'," he chuckled.

"Abortions are commonplace in China," continued Lenny. "The alternative is a heavy fine. People with more than one child often flee to another province so they cannot be traced and the husband will take on casual labouring jobs to feed his family. However, if he cannot find work, the family become beggars. Because they are no longer registered with the Government, there is no Social Security payment to fall back on."

"I've heard that the single Chinese child is treated like a prince and given the best education available," said Jane. "Is that true?"

"Education is very highly regarded so the child is given the best the parents can afford, with extra tuition in the evenings and at weekends," Lenny confirmed. "Private schools are very expensive but nonetheless, places are in great demand. Every parent wants their child to go to University."

He added, "In the past, the minority tribes were looked down on and despised by the Han majority but now they are given preferential treatment. Provided they marry within the tribe, they may have two children and these children are allowed to go to University with lower examination grades than the Han youngsters."

By this time, we had reached the outskirts of the market and we were passing food stalls and restaurants. Pots and pans were bubbling away on stoves at the front of the open dining areas while customers sat on plastic stools round small tables at the rear, waiting for their meals to be served.

Some of the cooks were offering a very limited supply of food but others had trestle tables laden with different types of meat, vegetables and salad, while fish swam in plastic bowls at the ends of the tables. We were beginning to feel hungry but it was not yet time for lunch. Lenny was now describing life as a member of the Yi tribe.

"Minority villages are located a long way from the cities," he said. "I remember, as a child, having to leave home at four o'clock in the morning to go to market with my mother, arriving at about midday. It was nearly midnight by the time we reached home again."

He started to tell us about some of the tribal customs. “Each tribe has its own traditions and religious beliefs which they try to preserve,” he said. “Some of the older people of the Yi tribe still believe that illness is caused by evil spirits. Rather than consult a doctor, they will burn paper and then drink the ashes mixed with water, to drive out the spirits harming them.”

As we entered the main market and passed a stall selling peacock feathers, Lenny told us, “Fifty years ago in the minority villages, it was normal to keep peacocks, like hens, for their eggs. There were once lots of peacock feathers in all the local markets but now they are comparatively rare.”

We came to a corner on which stood an attractive house. The open shop area was supported on concrete pillars but the upper living accommodation was still made of wood, painted green. Between the walls and the raised roof, where grass grew between the tiles, an opening suggested a loft storage and drying area.

We turned off into the street next to this house and reached a section of the market selling live birds, including brightly coloured yellow, green and blue budgerigars, packed tightly into cages and baskets. Other stalls sold very decorative bamboo cages as well as plainer metal ones.

“The Chinese love their birds,” said Lenny, although this was somewhat difficult to believe when they were crammed in so tightly together. “People often take them for walks in their cages and on a fine day, you will see cages hanging outside the windows of apartments to let the birds enjoy the fresh air.”

In the middle of the street, a man bent over a tube of polished bamboo, about eighteen inches long and three inches in diameter, supported in his left hand. His right hand was held over a short, narrow piece of bamboo which was attached at an angle to the larger tube, a few inches from the bottom.

"What's he holding?" asked Liz, a tall slim woman in her mid-twenties, with long brown hair that she wore in a single thick plait down her back.

"That's a cannabis pipe," answered Lenny. "You will find men smoking these everywhere. It's made from bamboo which is a very versatile plant. We use it for everything from food to furniture, from building frameworks of houses to tiling the roofs."

As we walked further into the market, Lucille saw a dagger with an ornamental handle. "Look," she said to Harry, "that would make a good present for Ricky."

"That's our grandson," Harry explained to those of us nearby. "Make sure it's blunt," he cautioned Lucille. "We don't want him cutting himself accidentally."

"Let me try and get a good price for you," offered David, once she had confirmed that it was suitable. He used his bargaining skills and got the price reduced for her from a hundred and twenty yuan to only nine yuan. Lucille was most impressed.

David's help was then enlisted by Liz's friend Jess, a buxom young woman in her mid-twenties who had short, light brown, wavy hair with blonde highlights. She wanted him to bargain for peacock feathers but this time, he was less successful. The stall holders obviously knew that somebody else would pay their price and were not so anxious to make a sale.

As we left the market area, we passed a shop outside which hung what appeared to be two very colourful wide-brimmed hats, each about two feet in diameter, made of paper flowers with gold foil butterflies on them. The bases of the crowns and the edges of the brims were ringed with white flowers although the concentric rings of flowers within the white bands varied in colour.

"What are those for?" asked Jess.

"They're what we use as funeral wreaths," Lenny replied.

It was now lunchtime and we were taken to a first floor restaurant at the side of the market. As we walked up the stairs, we passed shelves on which stood decorative bottles of alcohol, the liquid varying in colour from clear to amber.

"What are those things in the bottles?" asked Julie.

"They look like snakes," said Chris. Julie peered closer and shuddered.

"You're right," she said. "Look, you can see that one's head." Sure enough, coiled in the bottom of each glass container was a whole snake.

As usual, we all sat round two large tables and helped ourselves to food from a variety of dishes brought to us by the waiters and laid out on the Lazy Susan in the centre.

As we ate, we and the other diners were entertained by two young women singing Chinese songs. These included versions of 'Auld Lang Syne' and 'Jingle Bells,' both of which seemed to be enjoying great popularity in China.

Over lunch, our clothes dried out quite well but as we left the restaurant, the rain appeared to have set in for the afternoon. It was only about ten minutes walk to our next venue, the Yuantong Buddhist temple, but by the time we arrived there we were wet through again.

Funeral wreaths

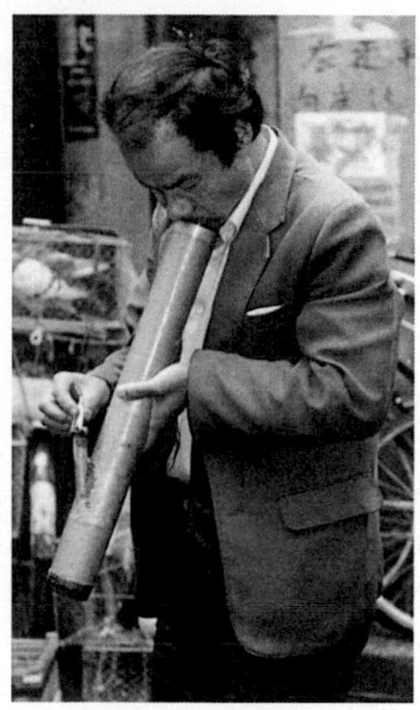

Cannabis pipe

Yuantong Temple gate

Yuantong Temple

From the entrance to the temple, we walked gently downhill along a wide paved path, lined with rows of potted red geraniums backed by neatly clipped low hedges, behind which grew a variety of trees.

In front of us stood an impressive entrance gate with three openings, the central upwards-curving bamboo roof overlapping the two side roofs. Above the central opening were four golden Chinese characters on a red background. Once we were through the gateway with the temple before us, we stopped while Lenny told us about its history.

"Yuantong is the oldest and most important Buddhist temple in Yunnan" he began. "It is also very unusual because, although you generally climb uphill to a Buddhist temple, you walk downhill to this one."

"The temple was first built in the eighth century AD but was demolished during the Mongolian wars led by Kublai Khan," he continued. "It was rebuilt in the early part of the fourteenth century during the Yuan Dynasty and has since been renovated and extended. While most temples were destroyed during the Cultural Revolution, Yuantong Temple survived because it was considered to be a historical monument. Yuantong is the Bodhisattva to whom the temple is dedicated."

Lenny then told us more about Yuantong. "He represents understanding and enlightenment and he looks down on the world with compassion," he said. "Because he found it impossible to cope with all the suffering on Earth, it is said that the Buddha arranged for Yuantong's head to be divided into many parts to enable him to hear the cries of all those who need his help and he was given a thousand arms to be able to reach out to them. You will recognise his statue inside the temple."

"Isn't the Government against religion?" asked Gordon. "I thought China was an atheist country."

"Since the 1970s, religion has not been suppressed," Lenny told us. "Not only have older people reverted to their previous religious practices but the young have also turned to religion in large numbers."

"Are most people either Buddhist or Taoist?" asked Liz.

"The main religions in China are Buddhism, Taoism and Confucianism, although Islam and Christianity are also important." Lenny looked around at us all. "This temple is always very busy so, if there are no further questions, I suggest that you now wander round on your own to see what you want. Meet me back here in half an hour."

David and I hurried off, anxious to see everything in the short time available. The temple was protected by two large, fierce guardian statues with golden faces and hands, bulging eyes and flowing black beards. They were dressed in colourful robes with red and blue predominating.

As we went through the buildings of the temple, we saw around the walls many statues of the Buddha and Bodhisattvas, including a golden statue of a many-armed but one-headed Yuantong. On either side of the main statue of Buddha were two tall pillars that, we were told, dated from the Ming Dynasty, each carved with a dragon, one gold and the other green.

In the main courtyard of the temple, people lit bundles of joss sticks at a fire burning in a large metal container under a canopy. They then held them upright in both hands while they prayed, letting the smoke carry their prayers up to the gods.

Separate stands held glowing red candles, standing on tiered shelves under canopies to protect them from the rain, and people were lighting their own candles from those already burning and adding them to the shelves. The smoke, added to the low cloud and mist around the compound, gave the place a wonderful atmosphere.

In the middle of the temple complex was a large pool of green water with a central island on which stood an octagonal, two tiered building, each tier with its own curving bamboo roof turning up at the corners. The roofs were a golden yellow, the walls were faded red and the upright pillars of the building were a brighter red, supporting a frieze under the eaves that was predominantly blue and green. These colours were repeated in the temple buildings around the pool.

The building was accessed over two white stone bridges, one on either side of the central island, each with three arches which reflected perfect circles in the pool below. It looked very picturesque.

The buildings round the outside of the temple held prayer rooms and exhibitions of photography and calligraphy. At the back of the temple, stone steps ascended the hill on either side but there was no time to find out where they led.

After the group met up again, we walked with Lenny back through the city to our hotel, where we had time to shower and change before going out as a group for our evening meal. We were then free for the rest of the evening and David and I went to explore more of Kunming.

The centre of the city with its tree-lined streets was like a larger, more prosperous version of Guilin with the same friendly, market town atmosphere but with more modern shops offering better quality goods.

As we were passing one open shop front, the two women behind the counter called to us and beckoned us over. We went across and they gestured at several bowls of a brown substance on the counter, inviting us to buy.

"Is that tobacco?" I queried. One of the women behind the counter grinned.

"No," she said. "You try."

I smelt it but did not recognise the scent. I then tasted it but was none the wiser. I shrugged my shoulders and raised my hands, palm upwards, in a gesture of ignorance.

"What is it?" I asked.

"Pot," she grinned.

"Oh. No, xie xie," I told her.

To the best of my knowledge, it was the first time I had seen cannabis. David laughed at me as we continued down the street.

"I didn't know you took drugs," he said. "Are you feeling all right?"

"You probably have to smoke it before it has any effect," I said.

After dark, we noticed that none of the bicycles had headlamps or reflectors which concerned us somewhat when we came to cross the roads. However, this was clearly normal and acceptable. When we adopted the usual practice of walking slowly and steadily across, the cyclists made their way around us and we found that there was no problem.

Saturday 16th October

The next morning, after breakfast, we left by coach to visit the Western Hills and Dragon Gate. As we crossed a railway line, Lenny drew it to our attention.

"That is the line to Burma, Vietnam and Laos. On completion, it was considered to be one of China's finest achievements but it was built at a high cost. Thirteen thousand men died during its construction."

As we neared Dragon Gate, we stopped in a large parking area and Austin told us, "At this point, we have to transfer from our coach to minibuses driven by men from the Hani tribe. In this part of Yunnan, the Hani minority tribe have their own reserved area in which they are permitted to do all the work available, in order to make a living."

On the other side of the parking area stood a row of very ancient, very dirty minibuses. Once we were on board, the driver of our particular bus had great difficulty in starting up the engine.

"It sounds as though the battery's nearly flat," I said.

Phil laughed. "Are you all ready to get out and push?"

We were beginning to think he may have a point when at last the engine caught and with a noisy crash of gears, we set off slowly uphill for about two miles, before stopping in an upper parking area where the rest of our group were waiting for us.

A file of workmen walked past us through the minibus park, each carrying a very large basket on his back from which protruded various tools.

However, we were more interested in the young Hani girls who stood in a small group, waiting to guide tourists up the mountain. They all looked small and dainty and were dressed in colourful outfits of embroidered knee-length cotton tunics over their trousers and knee-length jackets in pink, turquoise blue or lemon-green.

Round the front of their heads, each wore a broad colourful band of stiffened material patterned with horizontal stripes, their long dark hair hanging freely down their backs. Most of these hats had one or two points of material sticking up above the band.

Because Lenny was from a minority tribe, albeit the Yi rather than the Hani, he was allowed to lead our group up the mountain himself. As we set off through mist and light drizzle, we could just make out the outline of Lake Dian or Dianchi down below.

"Dianchi once covered an area of five hundred square miles," Lenny told us. "It was so large that it was like a sea and as they crossed it, many ships were lost in storms. Because the lake was so dangerous, one man, a Taoist monk, decided to create a Taoist temple on the mountain to appease the gods. He began to work alone in 1780 and after he had been labouring for fourteen years, carving out paths, steps and shrines, other people became so impressed with his efforts that they decided to help."

As he led us, single file, up a very narrow path and a series of steps, we passed a number of small shrines. Although these were protected by overhanging rock, some of the colours were so bright that I decided they must have been renovated recently by local artists.

We paused where the path opened out into a wider area near a carved dragon and Lenny told us, "Dragon Gate survived the Cultural Revolution because the local people hung the shrines with pictures of Mao. They told the Red Guards that Mao was worshipped here, so they were afraid to destroy the temple and shrines."

He then added, "In front of you is a dragon of fortune. If you touch its eyes, you will become rich."

Alan grinned and his eyes sparkled. He was a carpenter from Newark in his early fifties, with sandy coloured hair and moustache and a permanent twinkle in his eye.

"Well," he chuckled, "I can't miss an opportunity like that." He touched the dragon's eyes and said, "I'm now expecting to win a packet on the football pools when I get back home." We all queued up behind him to guarantee our future wealth.

As we climbed higher, the path became steeper and narrower. Luckily it was only being used as the uphill route because there was certainly no room for anyone to pass.

Many of the steps were in tunnels cut through the rock but in places, there were viewpoints above the lake and the scenery would have been lovely on a clear day. We paused again in another wider area, beside a rock carved with a phoenix, a box hanging from its beak.

"This place is known as Phoenix Rock or the Old Stone House," Lenny told us. "The monk climbed up the rock and built a shelter here. All of this path and the steps were chiselled out by hand and in places where the rock face was vertical, the monk had to hang from the top of the cliff on a chain to carve them out of the stone."

It was impossible to imagine such single-minded commitment and self-discipline over a period of fourteen years or more. One of the last shrines on the mountain was dedicated to a god that helped those taking examinations.

As we neared the top and were no longer walking round the side of the cliff, the path widened and we came across a woman sitting to one side selling slices of pineapple on sticks to refresh the weary visitors to the shrines. The pineapple pieces were latticed with holes and arranged on a plate, balanced on the base of an upturned bucket that had been used to carry the pineapples up the mountain. The woman was wearing red woollen gloves and using a small piece of wood to remove the seeds from the fruit and to make the holes.

"Do you think those gloves would be more or less hygienic than bare hands?" asked David.

"I wouldn't like to say," I replied, "but I don't think I'll risk eating any of that pineapple."

A little further up, the path took us under cables from which a chair was suspended and as we neared the top of the hill, we could see the terminus of a chair lift that was under construction.

"This should be completed by next year," Lenny said. "It will then be possible to ride up the mountain."

As we saw workmen trudging up the hill carrying baskets of sand and gravel on their backs, we realised that all the materials to construct the chair lift had to be brought up from the valley.

"Each labourer decides on the load he will carry in his basket," Lenny told us. "It is weighed at the top and he is then paid according to how much he has delivered."

Behind the chair lift, hazy through the light mist, we could see a pagoda silhouetted against the grey sky. As we climbed up to it, we found it was an open hexagonal viewing platform with a double upturned roof. However, the view from the platform consisted of little but mist and cloud. It had taken us about two hours to reach the top.

The route we took back down was paved and much less steep. It was also much wider and we passed many labourers lugging their loads to the top.

David and Lenny were chatting and getting on really well together. Lenny showed us a photograph of his fiancée, a beautiful Muslim girl.

"We have no particular religious beliefs," he said, "but her parents are against the marriage because I am not a Muslim."

"Is that going to be a problem?" asked David.

"No, we are both old enough to do what we want. These days, as in the West, it is becoming more common for couples to live together without bothering to get married. However, I want to do things properly so we will defy her parents and marry anyway."

Further down the mountain, David was talking to Lenny about the difficulties caused by drugs smuggled into China.

"Drugs are a big problem," Lenny agreed. "There are four clans of tongs who control the drug rackets and there is gang warfare in every large city as these tongs fight for supremacy."

The drizzle had now turned to rain and back at the upper car park, some of the Hani girls were sheltering under colourful umbrellas. We returned to the ancient minibuses for a short trip down to Huating Temple. This time, Lenny was in our vehicle and pointed out the Burma Road which snaked six hundred and twenty miles over the mountains to Burma.

Once we were all standing together outside the temple, Lenny explained why it was so important. “Huating Temple was built in the eleventh century for a high ranking Buddhist Lord as his summer residence,” he said. “It was he who first brought the Buddhist scriptures to this area from central China.”

We went up a flight of steps and through the entrance gate into the temple grounds. In the lower part of the complex lay a peaceful lake, where water lilies floated on the surface and a sculpture of worn limestone added interest at one end. Successive flights of steps then led us up the hillside to the various temple buildings.

On either side of the entrance to one of these were two huge and very ferocious looking guardian figures, each about ten feet tall above their pedestals.

“The one on the right represents fire and the one on the left represents water,” Lenny told us. Beside the fire guardian sat a quite cute-looking snarling dragon, while the water guardian was also supported by a snarling animal, which I guessed was a serpent. The bamboo roofs of the temple, some green, some gold, had the usual good luck figures along the lower edges of the up-curved corner copings.

The main pavilion had a two-tiered golden roof with red and gold lanterns hanging across the width of the structure from the lower eaves. In front of this was a stone paved courtyard where people were burning incense and paper offerings, the smoke carrying their prayers to heaven.

The courtyard was decorated with an extensive array of pots containing flowering plants and tiny conifers. The area was surrounded by mature evergreens and deciduous trees, their rich red and gold autumn colourings looking beautiful against the temple buildings and green backdrop of the hills.

After looking around Huating Temple, we had lunch in a building on the opposite side of the road before walking back to our coach. We were then driven to the outskirts of Cheng Gong, a village near Lake Dian, where the coach was parked again.

"We'll try and arrange a ride down to the lake," said Austin.

We were crossing a square in the centre of the village when Lenny paused. "Come and look at this," he suggested, walking over to a notice board. We followed and saw a selection of head and shoulder photographs pinned to the board.

"The Burma Road has always been used to bring drugs into China," Lenny observed, "and this is a warning not to get involved with them. The photographs show some of the drug traffickers who've been captured and paraded in front of the local people, before being put to death. In this province alone in the past five years, over three hundred people have been executed for dealing in drugs."

It was clear that the rewards had, at least partially, cancelled out the deterrent effect but without action, the drug problems may have been much worse.

At the far end of the market place, we found the local transport, a row of horse-drawn, two-wheeled covered carts.

"We're going to use three of these to take us down to the lake," said Austin. "Each cart should hold about eight people. There are twenty five of us altogether but if we can't all get in, Lenny has volunteered to stay behind and meet us back at the coach."

Somehow, we all managed to squeeze into the three carts and we set off at a trot towards the lake, two miles away. David and I had the two seats at the back of our cart and although we had the advantage of being able to look at the scenery, we had to hold on with both hands to avoid falling out, particularly when the cart lurched on the rough track.

The dirt road was lined with blue-green eucalyptus trees and ran beside a river that flowed into the lake. Women were washing their laundry in the water and we could see people working in the fields on the other side.

The drivers enjoyed racing their horses which made the hold on our seats even more precarious and, as the carts kept overtaking each other, we cheered whenever we appeared to be winning the race. Luckily, there was no other traffic on the road. When we reached the lake, Austin paid the drivers who returned with their transport to the village.

"When I've been here with previous tours," Austin told us, "I've tried without success to hire some of the local fishing boats to take us out on the lake. I'm hoping I might have better luck on this occasion."

We walked down to where the river flowed into the lake. At the mouth of the river, half a dozen boats were moored on the mud banks.

A cold wind was whipping up the waves so the lake looked like a rough sea and when we reached the boats, we found they were all half full of water.

Dragon Gate

Huating Temple

Farmer

Local transport

Canal crossing

We could understand why so many boats sank in storms on the lake and were relieved when Austin changed his mind about hiring these. We were more than happy to view Lake Dian from the shore.

Beside the lake ran a wall about a foot wide, the purpose of which was to prevent flooding. Austin decided that as we were not going out on the lake, we would walk along the wall instead, to see some of the local people at work in the fields. Luckily, the wall was in a good state of repair but there was a four foot drop to very boggy ground on one side and to the lake on the other side.

As we made our way unsteadily along the top of the wall, trying to gaze ahead rather than looking down, we passed fields divided into rectangular plots of very healthy-looking crops.

Here and there, a small copse of trees stood against the wall and from the branches of the trees hung dozens of very large, very colourful spiders with red backs and yellow and black striped legs. We did our best not to disturb these. We also spotted an enormous caterpillar, bright green and hairy, with a raised dark bar along each side and bright red globules, like small berries, attached to its head, sides and back which gave the impression that it would be lethal.

After about a mile of balancing along the wall, which changed height quite frequently, we had left the lake behind but had come to a drainage canal which was about nine feet across. It was spanned by a bridge, only about a foot wide, consisting of three logs tied together with nothing to hold on to.

"We haven't got to cross that, have we?" Mandy asked in horror.

"Don't worry," said Austin airily. "We'll help you over."

Austin crossed first and while Li Mei assisted each of us on to the bridge, he encouraged us over and gave us a hand to help us off on the other side. The bridge bounced uncomfortably as we crossed and David and I were relieved to make it without mishap. Mandy and Jenny refused to attempt the crossing until Lenny, who had a good sense of balance, led each of them over, holding both hands and walking backwards himself.

"Well done," said Austin, once we were all safely on the other side.

"My legs are shaking," said Mandy. "We don't have to walk along any more walls, do we?"

"No," Austin assured her. "We can take paths through the fields back to Cheng Gong."

There were several people working on their plots as we passed. We were unable to speak to them, other than to say "ni hau", and they were equally unable to converse with us. Nevertheless, they were all very friendly and held up their crops to show us with beaming smiles.

They each had one or two flat, long-handled baskets which they were filling with vegetables and salad crops for the market and probably for their own use as well. These baskets would be carried across their shoulders, slung from a bamboo pole.

While we were walking through the fields, Liz pointed out to Jess that the zip on her rucksack had broken, leaving it hanging open. Jess hurried forward to speak to Austin.

"Do you know of anywhere where I can get this repaired?" she asked him.

"Yes, there'll be someone who can do that in Cheng Gong market," he told her. "We'll stop there for a few minutes when we get back."

He had a word with Lenny and when we reached the village, Lenny took us down one of the side streets to a stall where there was a sewing machine. Lenny spoke to the stall holder, who was busy repairing bags and shoes.

After inspecting Jess's rucksack, the stall holder replaced the puller on the zip and restitched it where it was coming away. The whole job took between ten and fifteen minutes and the charge was three renminbi, which at that time was the equivalent of about twenty five pence. Jess was highly delighted.

We arrived back in Kunming during the evening rush hour to find weddings taking place everywhere.

"It's Saturday the sixteenth of October," explained Lenny. "The luckiest number in China is eight, which means wealth. Double numbers are also lucky so the sixteenth day of any month is a very propitious day to get married, although the most popular month is August." He added, "The Chinese are very superstitious and the most sought after car number in China is 12888 which means, 'I want to be very wealthy'."

"Why are all the brides dressed in red or pink?" asked Mattie.

"Again, this is superstition," said Lenny. "Red is a very lucky colour. I believe brides in Europe wear white to indicate purity but here, white is the colour of mourning." He added, "You'll probably hear firecrackers going off in the streets all night tonight. These are to celebrate and to scare off evil spirits."

As it was nearly five o'clock, we went directly to the restaurant where we would be eating that evening. Two tables had been reserved for us at the far end of a large room with a stage to one side. All the tables, including ours, were decorated with real flowers, the first we had seen in a restaurant in China that were not made of paper or plastic. Lenny informed us that the rest of the venue had been booked for a wedding party.

The wedding group arrived very shortly after us. We ordered our meal and while we waited for it to arrive, David went round trying to communicate with members of the wedding party and discovering that some of them could speak a few words of English. He identified the bride's parents and sister and Lenny then introduced him to the bride and groom, who happened to be friends of his.

"Now you have met the newly-weds," said Lenny, "you must go up on the stage to make a speech."

"You're joking," David said, shocked.

"No, I'm not, it's the custom." Lenny then went up on stage himself, introduced a very reluctant David to all the other guests in Chinese and handed him the microphone with an encouraging grin.

David rose to the occasion brilliantly and made a short speech, saying how we were all honoured to be present at the wedding reception and wishing the young couple a long and very happy life together. Lenny translated his words into Chinese, everybody clapped and our group was then treated as part of the wedding party.

As David came back to our table, Austin said, "Well done. We were all very surprised to see you up on stage. How did that happen?"

"Lenny introduced me to the bride and groom and then told me I had to make a speech. I had no choice," David told him.

Our meal had just been served when the wedding entertainment started and continued for the rest of the evening. There were singers, dancers, acrobats and jugglers.

Shortly after we had finished eating, a bridesmaid came round with a silver tray of sweets and cigarettes. Lenny spoke to her and then said, "You are invited to take two items each from the tray."

I chose two sweets, one in a pink wrapper with pictures of Kung Fu fighters on it, the other in a yellow wrapper with pictures of blue convolvulus called 'Flower's Kiss Sweets', and put both in my pocket for later. The best man then came across and filled our glasses with a very sweet red wine.

"This is to toast the bride and groom when they come to our table," Lenny told us.

The happy couple had to visit each table in turn and drink a toast with their guests. As ours were the fifteenth and sixteenth tables, they were looking quite glassy-eyed by the time they reached us and the groom was staggering slightly as we wished them long life and happiness.

It was after midnight by the time we returned to our hotel but the streets of the city were still full of revellers letting off firecrackers. When we finally fell asleep in the early hours of the morning, it was to the background noise of fireworks, sounding like machine gunfire.

5

The Stone Forest

Sunday 17th October

The alarm went off at seven o'clock the next morning and we staggered out of bed, bleary-eyed, to get ourselves ready for breakfast and to pack everything we would need for the next three days into our small rucksacks. Our main luggage had to be outside our rooms by eight o'clock, ready to be transferred to a hotel in Emei, where we would next see it on Tuesday evening.

After breakfast, we set off in the coach with our rucksacks on our knees. Because the average Han Chinese was of a smaller build than the average Westerner, the space allowed on local coaches was 'snug' to say the least and with our backpacks being more full than usual, there was insufficient room to put them down between our feet.

Our first visit that morning was to a Sunday Market out in the countryside. When we stopped, Austin said, "You can leave your overnight bags on your seats. Just take your cameras and money with you. The coach will be locked and the driver will stay here to look after things." He told us the time to be back at the coach and we went off by ourselves to explore.

When Austin told us we were going to see yet another market, my first reaction had been that I had already seen enough markets to satisfy my curiosity. Once we started walking round, however, I discovered that this one was well worth the visit. Crowds of people came from miles around to sell their produce and their skills and to buy.

Fruit, vegetables and salads appeared to be of even better quality than we had seen elsewhere. One salad stall was heaped high with long Cos-type lettuces and huge red radishes, many over a foot long, beside another crop with long straight bushy leaves criss-crossing into a white ridged stem with a pointed orange tip. Tomatoes came in all sizes and ranged in colour from ripe red to green with just a hint of yellow. A customer purchased some of these and we watched as they were weighed in a metal bowl hung from a hand-held balance bar.

There were several types of fungi, some flat and plate-like, others in clusters that seemed to grow outwards in all directions from a central point.

To one side of the fruit, vegetable and salad stalls sat a whole row of shoe repairers and bag menders, most of whom were busy with customers.

There was a livestock area with ducks, chickens, rabbits, guinea pigs and gerbils. Nearby were baskets full of duck and chicken eggs and sacks full of very tiny eggs.

"What are those?" I asked Li Mei, who was walking round the market with me and David.

"Those are quails' eggs."

We saw no large animals for sale in the Sunday Market and apart from small items like chickens' feet, there was very little butchered meat. However, several stalls were selling large quantities of fat.

"Do people eat a lot of fat meat?" I queried.

"No," Li Mei laughed. "Most of it will be rendered down for cooking."

Fresh bread rolls were being produced in large shallow steamers and Li Mei bought a couple of these. She ate one as she was walking round and gave us the other one to share between us. It looked a little like a very large, smooth scone and had a soft, doughy texture, quite unlike European bread and with no flavour of yeast.

In a shallow pan on one stall were what looked like pieces of coconut ice, each about two inches by three inches across and about two and a half inches deep. The lower two inches were white, covered by a layer of deep pink. Between these were larger slabs, the golden brown colour of a syrup sponge but drier and firmer in texture. Li Mei told us that the pink and white items were made of rice while the golden brown blocks were made of wheat.

We came to a stall covered in very angular woody stems on which were tiny black berries.

"Would you like to taste those?" asked Li Mei.

"No, thank you," said David, who was not feeling very adventurous, food-wise.

The stall holder offered me a twig a couple of inches long from which sprouted five side branches and on which were four of the little black fruits. "Xie xie," I said, smiling at her and accepting it. I tried the berries and found they were like miniature bilberries but were nearly all pip with very little flesh.

"Do you like them?" asked Li Mei. "They are very good for your health."

"Yes, thank you," I said. "They are very sweet but very small."

They may also have been very nutritious but to my mind, not worth the effort of eating them. The stall holder hopefully held out a pan of the fruit but I shook my head with a smile and said "xie xie" again.

A nearby stall was selling long slabs of a white substance. "Is that cheese?" I asked Li Mei.

"It is not possible to buy cheese in China," she said. "The Han people think of it as milk which has curdled and gone bad. That is bean curd."

Further on was a yellow cake which Li Mei told us was made from soya beans. We then came to a stall selling a dark brown substance, shaped as though it had been poured into shallow rounded bowls with sloping sides to solidify.

"Those are cakes of sugar made from beet," explained Li Mei. "They are to use in cooking."

It began to rain and umbrellas went up as we reached an area selling lengths of bamboo. In this part of the market, there were also woven baskets. These ranged in size from the shallow trugs with long handles that we had seen in our walks across the fields to the hip-high baskets, both oval and round in shape, from which we had seen farmers selling their larger crops in the markets. There were shopping baskets in all shapes and sizes and a separate pile of woven trays and mats. There was a rush to cover everything over with sheets of polythene, as protection from the weather.

A young woman walked past us carrying a baby in a brightly embroidered cloth bag on her back. Later, we were able to watch as another young mother fastened her baby into position. It looked a precarious procedure.

The woman bent forward and literally threw the baby on to her back. While it balanced there, she used both hands to throw a small blanket over it. She then fastened some string across the bottom of the blanket, tied it round her waist at the front and brought up the ends of the string to fasten to the top corners of the blanket over her shoulders, which held the container tight down both sides. As she stood upright, the baby dropped down safely into its bag. This particular child's head was completely hidden by the blanket but the head of a larger child would have poked out of the top.

We now walked to the edge of the market where a man stood against a brick wall wearing an oculist's mirror on a metal band round his head. On the ground stood a black brief case beside which was a white cloth covered with the tools of his trade and a couple of reference books.

"That's the ear cleaner," Li Mei told us. "If you're going deaf, he will remove the wax from your ears." It was apparently not considered necessary to soften the wax first.

Further along the wall stood a selection of bamboo cannabis pipes, some varnished a light, natural colour, or stained a rich dark brown with four decorative bands in black or metallic silver, others painted white and decorated with four bands of colour, green, brown, blue and red. Cannabis and tobacco were being sold on the next stall and men were apparently trying out the pipes before deciding whether to buy.

"About a third of the men in this province smoke," remarked Li Mei. "The majority smoke tobacco but pot smoking is also very common. Women generally do not smoke."

Either the pot or the tobacco smoking, probably both, was no doubt responsible for the horrible habit of noisily clearing the throat before spitting out phlegm that we were coming across everywhere we went in China.

We had now reached the far end of the market. Beyond the stalls was a small stream and on the opposite side, in a small grassy area surrounded by tall brick buildings, were dozens of carts with grazing horses still harnessed to them. At least they had food and water while they waited for their owners to return.

We now started to make our way back round the other side of the market and almost immediately came upon a rather gruesome stall, along the front of which lay half a dozen dead rats. Behind them were some large plastic sachets, some containing a bright yellow liquid, others containing a bright red liquid. To one side were some cardboard containers, each about the size of a small box of chocolates and each holding about two dozen tiny phials of coloured liquid, one box having red phials, another with green and yellow ones. At the other end of the table were sachets of powder. There were also some wooden mouse traps.

"That man sells rat poison," Li Mei grinned, as she saw the looks on our faces. "The dead rats are to show how efficiently it works."

We stopped for a short while to watch a shoe and bag repairer at work. A customer had broken the wide strap on her plastic shopping bag and the man rummaged through his selection of patches to find an exact colour match. He then found a corresponding yarn, threaded his sewing machine and double stitched round the repair patch in just a few minutes while the customer waited. When he had finished, the repair was almost invisible.

Just beyond him, a barber was at work. He had erected an awning above a folding chair to keep his customers dry and a man was seated facing the wall, while the barber shaved his head with a cut-throat razor.

We then came to the dentist. He had a small table covered with a red cloth on which he had placed a white covered tray for his instruments, a bag of cotton wool, a variety of containers and bottles, a selection of about fifty very white false teeth (although there was no indication as to how they would be fitted), some wax for impressions and, at the front of the table, a pile of about a hundred yellowing teeth that had been extracted.

As we passed, the dentist was hard at work, using a pair of long-handled pliers to tug at one of the teeth of a brave young patient, who was standing behind the table. We hurried past quickly, not wanting to see any more.

It was now time to rejoin our friends and make our way back to the coach. We had all found the market absolutely fascinating.

As we set off again, Austin announced that our next stop would be for one of the compulsory factory visits, this time to a jade factory. A few miles further on, we crossed a single track railway line.

"That's the main line from China to Vietnam," Austin said, pointing it out to us. "Trains travel along there at walking pace for a distance of about six hundred miles."

At the jade factory, the lumps of raw jade looked grey and uninteresting while the finished articles on sale were lovely but, as usual on a factory visit, very expensive. However, we enjoyed looking at them.

Apart from the jade, there were some marquetry portraits of women which I liked very much and some very ornate quilted and embroidered pictures studded with glass beads and with beaded frames. One particularly gaudy one showed a phoenix confronting a dragon.

There were also paintings said to be by a local artist, mostly of flying cranes or tigers which were quite good or of very stylised mountain scenery which were not so good. However, we had seen almost identical paintings elsewhere.

"There seems to be a very limited range of subjects and styles in Chinese art," I said to David.

"The originals were probably by famous artists and all the other artists simply copy them," he agreed.

We discovered that a set of four small paintings representing the four seasons cost £250 each or £600 for the set. They all looked very similar with a precipitous blue-green mountain, rounded at the top, dark blue-green trees, a grey-green lake with some tiny boats on it and pavilions with upturned roofs, much too large for the proportions of the scenery. The summer picture had a splash of red in it, the autumn picture had some vivid orange to represent the autumn tints and the winter picture had less blue-green and more white. I was not impressed.

A coach load of Japanese visitors had arrived shortly before us and were receiving all the attention. The sales assistants had probably learned from experience that they were more likely to spend a fortune than an English group. Consequently, we were given a pot of cold tea and some peanuts and were left to our own devices.

When we had been there looking around for long enough to satisfy the authorities, we set off again towards the Stone Forest. The rain that had started when we were in the Sunday market had now developed into an unrelenting downpour and we were glad we were on the coach.

The soil in this area was in bands of deep red and yellow, probably clay and rich in minerals. Then, for a distance of several miles, the hills closed in and the road followed a river through a narrow, winding, steep-sided valley that reminded me of Cheddar Gorge but was far more extensive. People appeared to be living in caves along the river bank.

Further along, the valley widened out and we came to an area famous for its roast duck. All along the river banks were flocks of white ducks and we passed a local bus with about twenty live white ducks standing on the roof. They must have been tied down but they looked as though they were just hitching a lift.

As we reached the village where we were having lunch, we saw rows of ducks, plucked ready for cooking, hanging by their necks from metal rails outside the houses. Rounded clay ovens with metal lids on top and roaring fires inside were spread out along the pavement.

"The ovens are fuelled with pine logs which give off a lot of heat," Austin told us. "The ducks are hung round the top edge of the ovens, above the flames, and are roasted within twenty minutes. You can try one for yourselves."

After our walk round the Sunday Market and our visit to the jade factory, we were now feeling hungry. The coach was parked at the roadside and, with eager anticipation, we walked to one of the many restaurants for our roast duck lunch. We were to be disappointed.

The meal started with a thin, oily watercress and marrow soup. We were then given a large bowl of sticky white rice and a single duck, chopped up on a plate, webbed feet and head, eyes, beak and all, to share between twenty five of us.

As we each tried to find a piece of meat to transfer to our bowls with our chopsticks, we discovered that the duck was all bone and skin with hardly any flesh and we each had only one or two tiny pieces to go with the dry rice. We left the restaurant still hungry and feeling that roast duck was greatly over-rated. Nevertheless, it was an interesting experience.

Our next stop was at Seven Star Village, occupied by the Sani minority tribe. We had donned our waterproofs and alighted from the coach in a torrential downpour. As we turned off the main road on to the raised concrete path that led through the village and watched the coach driving away, wc decided that we must all be slightly crazy.

As Lenny led us through the village, we found it had character and would have looked very picturesque on a sunny day. The houses were built of mud brick with bamboo tiled roofs and many had balconies or open upper floors where washing was hung to dry under the shelter of the eaves. Bunches of peppers hung down the walls while maize and rice grains were spread out on cloths on the ground, in the forlorn hope that they would eventually dry.

Windows were simply holes in the wall with no glass although some had wooden bars across them. All the front doors stood open and each had pictures of a guardian god, with Chinese characters alongside, hung across the lintel and down each side frame. Through one of these doorways, we could see women sitting on the floor, stringing tobacco leaves together, ready to be hung up inside to dry.

Lenny led us through the village to the Sani primary school. In the middle of its central courtyard stood a stone table tennis table. A blackboard covered in characters stood on an easel outside, under the shelter of an overhanging roof.

"The children attend school six days a week, Monday to Saturday, from eight in the morning until twelve noon and from two until four o'clock in the afternoon," said Lenny. "Written on the blackboard are maths problems and general knowledge questions for them to work on when they arrive."

As we continued through the village, the path curved back to the main road past the cemetery, where we paused to look at the graves.

"The headstones are horseshoe-shaped and all face east which is the most propitious direction," explained Lenny. "There is a carved metal back-plate on the graves of the richest people. These take many years to complete and anyone dying unexpectedly from an accident or illness would have no back-plate."

Back at the main road, we had to wait about twenty minutes for the coach to come and pick us up and by the time we climbed on board, the rain had penetrated our waterproofs and we were all soaked to the skin. We reached our hotel at five o'clock and found it was cold.

Seven Star Village

Stone Forest

It was run by the Sani and was very basic with no heating in any of the rooms. However, David and I were relieved to find that our en-suite had a water heater over the bath so at least we were able to wash in hot water.

"I'm wet through," he said. "Are you going to put your dry clothes on?"

"We only have one change of socks and underwear each," I said. "They'll get damp from our wet trousers and shoes if we wear them now. I'm saving mine for tomorrow."

I hung up the dripping anoraks and when I had wrung the excess water out of our other clothes, we put them on again to dry with what was left of our body heat.

We only had a few minutes before going down for the evening meal. At least the food was hot. When we ordered our drinks, David bought a bottle of rice wine which he saved.

After we had finished eating, we went through to the small lounge where the seating consisted of long wooden benches. We all squeezed on to these, huddling close together for warmth as we were all shivering. While we talked, David passed round the rice wine which tasted terrible but warmed our blood.

A Japanese group was also staying in the hotel and after the meal, they went to the karaoke bar – every hotel in China had one – where they sang very loudly and off key until eleven o'clock. Then complete silence fell, for the first and only night that we spent in China. After a hot bath to warm us through before going to bed, David and I slept really well.

Monday 18th October

We were up early and were pleased to discover that our clothes had almost dried out overnight.

Austin and Lenny had agreed that we should leave the hotel at a quarter past eight, to visit the Stone Forest before the tour groups arrived. We were down in the dining room at half past seven for breakfast but the Sani staff were clearly not accustomed to early risers.

Austin went to chase them up and by eight o'clock two teapots had arrived, one containing tea, the other containing coffee. With them was a can of very sweet condensed milk. We all poured out a drink of one or the other and a few minutes later, the Sani women brought in some sponge cake and some very sweet bread rolls, which had jam in the centre like doughnuts. As we ate these with our hot drinks, we could hear cooking going on behind a screen.

"We shall have to be going soon," said Austin.

"Can't we just hang on for a few more moments," begged Chris. "I'm longing for a hot hard-boiled egg." This was something that had been served at several of our previous hotels.

"O.K.," agreed Austin, "provided it's ready by a quarter past eight and you're happy to eat it as you're walking along."

At a quarter past eight precisely, the staff brought in a plate of pickled cabbage and some watery cabbage soup. "That's it," said Austin and we all left the dining room together, leaving the women looking at us open-mouthed in amazement.

After hurrying back to our rooms to grab whatever we needed for the day, we left the hotel only five minutes later than planned. Although the air felt damp and the ground was wet, it was not actually raining for which we were thankful.

As we walked towards the Stone Forest, we passed a group of villagers buying their vegetables and salads from a small roadside market. Some vegetables had been spread out on cloths on the ground but most of them were still in the baskets in which they had been carried from the fields that morning. We then came to another Sani village.

"This is Five Tree village," Lenny told us. "The particular five trees after which the village was named were all cut down during the Cultural Revolution. Many Sani buildings were also destroyed and reconstructed in the plain Han style. This village is built on the very edge of the Stone Forest, which is of great religious significance to the Sani tribes."

Although the houses were generally less attractive than those in Seven Star, the village itself stood on the side of a hill with trees and shrubs growing on either side of the concrete path and between the buildings. As in Seven Star village, corn cobs and peppers were hanging from the eaves or strung from poles to dry. Near one of the houses were some beautiful sleek black pigs in a wooden pen.

"These animals were once kept on the ground floor of the house with the living quarters above," said Lenny. "They are now kept at the side of the house."

"People in some European countries still keep their animals under the living quarters of their houses during the winter," said Julie, while Lenny looked at her in utter disbelief. We assured him that she was correct.

Some of the Sani women came outside to try to sell us hand-embroidered hats, aprons, money belts and tablecloths. David and I glanced at the items but apart from the fact that we needed to change money and only had thirty renminbi left, we really did not want anything. As we left the village, we could see grey rock outcrops on the other side of a very overgrown lake.

"The Stone Forest is made up of vertical pinnacles of limestone containing many marine fossils," said Lenny. "From a distance, the rocks are said to resemble a forest of trees, which is where the name comes from. Normally, only the Sani are permitted to take people round the area but as the Sani are related to the Yi tribe, I am allowed to be your guide."

As we entered the Stone Forest, we came to a clearing.

"This is the Sani Festival ground," Lenny told us. "This is where they give displays of folk dancing, wrestling and bull fighting. From here, the paths are a concrete maze between the rocks and I must ask you to keep together as you could very easily become lost."

The paths and steps were very wet and slippery but young girls were sweeping them with twig brooms to keep them clear of leaves. The Sani girls wore almost identical clothing to the Hani guides we had seen at Dragon Gate, except that their coats were even brighter, in luminous shades of pink and green, with inset panels of yellow or turquoise.

Concrete picnic tables and stools had been provided wherever there was enough space but these failed to detract from the magnificent grandeur of the rocks which towered to about twenty feet above our heads. Most of the rocks had vertical sides, some with arches eroded through them. Many were fluted and some had smaller chunks of limestone balanced precariously on their topmost points, looking as though they could fall at any moment.

At first, we appeared to have the Stone Forest to ourselves and there was time to linger, take a photograph and then catch up with the others. Paths and steps led off in all directions and it would be very easy to lose our way. Then the coach parties arrived and kept crossing through and intermingling with our group so that life became much more difficult and we each had to ensure that we were following the right person.

The Sani guides were all lovely young girls. Lenny knew most of them and when a group stood at a higher level looking down on us, the Sani leader would wave to him.

When we reached a wider area where we could stop, Lenny gave us a wicked grin and said, “You may have noticed that many of the girls have points of material on their hats.” We nodded. “If there are two points, one facing up, the other facing down, the girl is single. If both points face upwards, she is engaged and if there are no points, she is married. Be very careful not to touch one of these hats,” he warned us. “If a man touches a point on a girl’s hat, this is seen as a proposal of marriage or, alternatively, is such an insult that the man would have to flee the country to escape the wrath of her family.”

As in the Reed Flute caverns, the Chinese had given these rocks names such as Sword Peak and the names were painted on the rocks in red Chinese characters. Lenny stopped us beside one of the tall pointed rocks that was broader at the base.

"This rock is hollow and echoes like a drum when you tap it. Listen," he said, demonstrating. The reverberating boom was unexpected and few of us could resist the temptation to rap on the rock as we passed it.

In one place, the path was very narrow and we had to squeeze between the rocks.

"If you can get through without touching the rocks on either side, you will live to be a hundred," Lenny laughed. Liz, who was just in front of me, managed it but I accidentally put a hand on one of the rocks as I inched in between.

We made our way to the highest point, which had a pavilion from where we could look down over the Stone Forest. Although the paths and steps had mostly seemed devoid of greenery, there was a surprising amount of foliage between the rocks when seen from above. Our walk around this area had been most enjoyable but we were unable to stay longer, as we had to get back to the hotel and be ready to leave by eleven o'clock.

Once on the coach again, we headed northwards, back to Kunming. On the way, another factory visit was scheduled, this time to a jade and carpet factory where all the workers were disabled, unable to hear or speak. We saw some half-worked jade and some half-finished carpets but it was now just after midday and all the workers were on their lunch break.

"The Chinese are very time-conscious," Lenny grinned. "At twelve noon, you can watch as all the workers in the fields down tools together and head home for lunch in a long line."

After five minutes, we were on our way again. Shortly after we left the factory, the coach drove slowly past a funeral procession. Everybody was dressed in white and wearing a white hat as a sign of mourning. One mourner carried a pole bearing three gold crowns, one above the other, while several of the other mourners carried huge brightly-coloured paper flower 'wreaths', similar to those we had seen in Kunming.

As we continued on our way, Lenny decided to tell us about some of the local Yunnan food specialities. We now suspected that Lenny liked to tease us, so we were not sure whether what he described was actually eaten or whether he was joking, but it made us feel quite ill.

We were not too surprised when he told us about eating raw meat or bees cooked in sauce. He then described eating the brains of monkeys, cut out while the animals were still alive and held in a clamp.

"Don't they do something like that in India?" queried Phil.

"You're thinking about that Indiana Jones film," laughed Jane.

Lenny chuckled and then, with great relish, described the 'three squeak' meal of live baby mice.

"They give one squeak when you pick them up in your chopsticks, a second when you dip them in soy sauce and the third when you pop them into your mouth," he said, giggling at the horrified looks on our faces. Ugh!

Having successfully put us off the idea of food, Lenny took us straight to a restaurant when we arrived in Kunming. Around the entrance were shelves holding bottles of snake wine, similar to those we had seen in the restaurant near the market on the previous Friday.

"You should try it," said Lenny with a grin, knowing that we were most unlikely to do so. "It's a very popular drink in Kunming. Snake blood is said to improve the eyesight and cure eye problems."

The restaurant turned out to be equipped for karaoke and as we ate, we were entertained by singers of very mixed ability from among the other diners. We had the usual Chinese version of 'Auld Lang Syne' and an Australian lady was persuaded to give a rather tuneless rendering of 'Jingle Bells'.

Towards the end of our meal, Lenny went up on the stage and sang us a Chinese farewell song with a great deal of emotion and tears began to run down his cheeks. Over the past few days, he had become a good friend and we all applauded him wildly.

He remained at the restaurant when we left and each of us shook his hand or gave him a hug and a kiss and he was presented with an unusually thick tips envelope. We were going to miss him.

From the restaurant, we were taken to a four star hotel for an hour before going to the railway station to take a train to Emei. Much to our relief, David and I were able to change some money here, but only by enlisting the help of the Assistant Manager and pretending that we would be returning to the hotel after our visit to Emei. To ease our consciences, we spent some of our newly obtained FECs at the hotel and bought a coffee each before visiting the hotel shop.

"I'd like some bottled water for the journey and some postcards," I said to David. "I can write them on the train."

We had already discovered that in China, postcards only came in packs of ten and each pack always contained several cards I did not like. I spent a little while sorting through the various packs before selecting one showing views of the Stone Forest. While I was choosing the cards, David was looking to see what else was on offer.

"Look," he said excitedly. "Bars of chocolate!" It was the first chocolate we had seen since we arrived in China.

"Wonderful," I said. "We'll buy a couple of bars to keep us going." We made our purchases and packed them into the rucksacks.

We were taken to the station with plenty of time to spare and the station master unlocked the door to the first class waiting room for us. We were honoured. The room had a carpet and padded chairs so we were able to wait for our train in comfort. Alan peered through a window into the adjacent waiting room.

"Hey, come and look at this," he said.

We all joined him and saw that this room was even more luxurious than ours, with a thicker looking carpet; chandeliers; and anti-macassars on the chair backs.

"That must be for the use of Communist Party officials," decided Austin.

We stayed in the waiting room until the train was pulling in to the platform. Austin found our carriage, the fourth out of twelve, and we climbed aboard with our rucksacks. We had been booked into a soft sleeper carriage which had compartments connected on one side by a corridor, in which there were a few folding wooden seats beside the windows.

Each compartment had two upper and two lower bunks with enough headroom for passengers to sit upright on the lower bunks during the day. Beside the window was a small table beneath which were two large insulated containers of hot boiled water. David and I were sharing our compartment with Austin and Li Mei.

During the rest of the afternoon, we visited each other's compartments and sat on the seats in the passageway, chatting and looking at the scenery where pink and white Japanese anemones grew wild along the railway embankments.

Most of the time, we travelled through valleys where the land was cultivated and sheltered by mountains that looked grey in the damp misty weather. Although we were now further north and the sun was setting later, in the gloom it was nearly dark by the time we went for dinner at six o'clock.

On the way to the dining car, we walked through a hard seat carriage. We saw that each compartment had three fixed wooden bunks on either side with insufficient headroom for sitting. The occupants had to travel lying on their bunks with a thin blanket over them, sitting on the few seats in the corridor or standing. We were glad Austin had arranged for us to travel in a little more luxury.

When we reached the dining car, we found small tables against the windows on one side, each set for four people. David and I were sharing with Jane and Phil.

Each table was draped with a white plastic cloth and decorated with a vase of brightly coloured plastic flowers but covering the flowers was a very dirty polythene bag, stapled round the stems.

"I wonder what the polythene bag is for," I said.

"I guess it's to prevent the passengers stealing the flowers," said Phil.

Just then, Austin came across to us.

"There's no choice of food, but I've ordered the set meal of cabbage soup, rice and chicken for us all."

"That sounds good," Jane decided. While we were waiting for our meal, the waiter brought a bowl of salad and placed it in the middle of the table.

"Ugh! What's that?" exclaimed Jane as something crawled on to the cloth.

As we watched, a variety of creatures left the bowl of salad and began making their way across the table. There were slugs and worms, caterpillars and beetles. We giggled and placed bets on what would reach the edge of the table first. Needless to say, we left the salad untouched.

When the soup arrived, it was hot and reasonably tasty and the chicken that was served with the rice was excellent. Instead of the ninety eight per cent bone, two per cent meat to which we had become accustomed, the chicken legs had meat on them and amazingly, there were even squares of chicken breast meat with no bone.

After the meal, Julie and Chris came to our compartment with a pack of cards and we taught Li Mei how to play rummy while she taught us a Chinese card game. We shared our bars of chocolate and although Li Mei declined, Julie and Chris were happy to have a few pieces.

We were then joined by Liz and Anna and the seven of us played 'Chase the Lady' with forfeits. Some of these forfeits required us to act in such a way that, had any Chinese passengers walked through our carriage, they would have been convinced that we were totally demented.

At eleven o'clock, the others returned to their compartments and, having had a perfunctory wash and cleaned our teeth in the tiny toilet areas at the end of the carriage, we settled on our bunks to sleep. David and I each had an upper bunk and found that these were firm but comfortable, each with a duvet and single pillow. We were soon lulled to sleep by the rhythmic sound of the train wheels clacking along the track.

Austin was drinking with some of the group in another compartment until the early hours and we saw nothing of him until the next morning, when he looked rather the worse for wear.

6

Emei

Sichuan Province

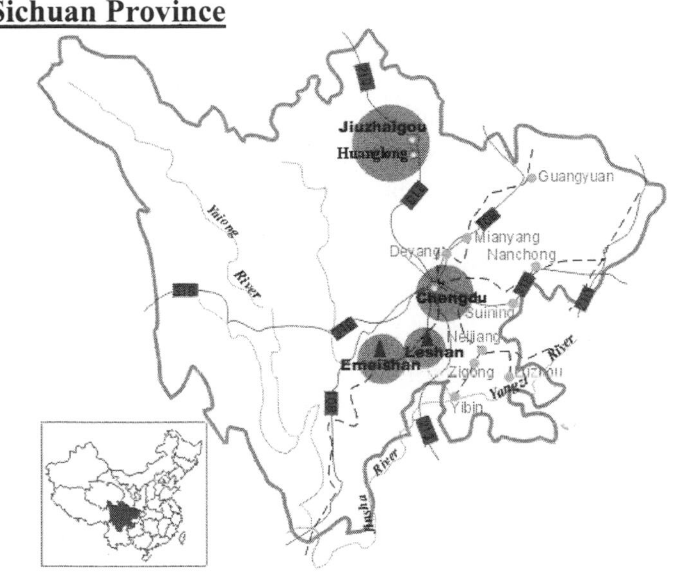

Tuesday 19th October

We were woken at a quarter past six with gentle piped Chinese music. Something in our meal the previous evening had upset me and also John, who had been seated at the next table. Overnight, we had both gone down with diarrhoea and sickness, although nobody else seemed to be affected.

As I did not feel like eating, I stayed in my bunk until the others went for breakfast and I was then able to use the toilet compartment without queuing. When David came back, he said, “You didn’t miss much darling. All we were given was watery rice soup, a greasy fried egg and pickled cabbage.”

All that morning, the train travelled through spectacular mountain scenery. For part of the journey, we followed a river that Li Mei told us was a tributary of the Yangtse. At midday, the others went through to the dining car for lunch and afterwards, David reported that Anita had found a large worm in the middle of her cabbage.

At a quarter past one that afternoon, we arrived at Emei in Sichuan Province, where we left the train. It was so much easier not having cases to worry about. At the end of the platform, we met our new local guide, a small dark man in his late twenties.

“Welcome to Emei, the location of one of China’s four sacred mountains,” he said. “My name is Yin Hao. It means hero.” He led us out to our waiting coach and we were driven to our hotel.

Emei town was similar in appearance to Kunming, except that all the street lights were blue and there were large statues on the islands in the centre of the road. Instead of going round these islands in a clockwise or anticlockwise direction, the traffic passed in both directions on either side.

Our hotel, on the outskirts of Emei, was built around two courtyards and was very attractive. Our cases were waiting for us in our rooms and we were free for the rest of the afternoon. Having spent the night on the train, the first thing David and I wanted was a hot bath and a change of clothes. We then felt ready to explore and went down to the hotel reception to see whether they had a map.

"This is the only one we have," said the woman behind the desk. She gave us a leaflet folded into six which, when opened out, gave a pictorial diagram of the mountain showing several different routes to the top.

There was a long outer route that was mainly footpath and several shorter routes that were mainly steps. These were clearly indicated on the map, which also gave the names of the various cliffs, ravines, caves, temples and rest houses to be found along the way, with pictures of the buildings. One highly improbable name, at a height of two thousand and seventy metres, was the Elephant Bathing Pond. It was a map to treasure.

Near the top of thc mountain were seven rocky buttresses, five of which had a temple or rest house beside the path to the summit. The first of these was marked as the Reception Hall at a height of two thousand five hundred and forty metres. The second was only named in Chinese characters but the third was called Cloudy Hospice. The fourth building was situated between the Golden Summit and the Thousand Buddha Summit at three thousand and seventy seven metres.

A small building, probably a viewing pavilion, was shown on the edge of the cliff at the highest point, on the Ten Thousand Buddhas Summit, at a height of three thousand and ninety nine metres.

David did a quick calculation. “That’s more than ten thousand feet,” he said.

Austin had told us on the train that morning that we would be climbing Mount Emei, Emeishan, the following day but when we saw the height of the mountain on the map, we realised that we would certainly not be going all the way to the top.

That afternoon, neither of us particularly wanted to walk down into Emei town because we both felt we had seen the best of it from the coach on the way to the hotel. However, after so long on the train, we needed to stretch our legs so we decided to walk to Baoguo Temple, at the foot of the mountain. Although the map indicated heights rather than distances, it showed that the temple, at five hundred and fifty metres, was only seventy five metres higher than Emei town.

The weather was grey and overcast but dry and we enjoyed the exercise. As it turned out, Baoguo Temple was only about half a mile uphill from the hotel.

The temple was fairly plain compared to others we had seen but for us it was memorable because the people we met there were all very friendly and wanted to practise their English on us. David started talking to an elderly Japanese man who was touring the area.

“Will you be climbing Emeishan while you are here?” the gentleman enquired.

“We shall be going up part of the way tomorrow,” said David.

“Then you must take my walking stick,” said our new friend, holding it out to my husband. It was made from an attractive polished wood with carving on the handle.

"I can't accept that. Surely you need it," David demurred.

"You will have more need of it when you climb the mountain," the elderly man insisted. "I have another walking stick at my hotel."

David thanked him for his generosity and told him that he was honoured by the gift and would make good use of it.

That evening, David ate with the others at the hotel while John and I sat in the Reception area. Our stomachs were still upset and neither of us could face the thought of eating. We chatted for a while and then I bought another pack of ten postcards from the hotel shop and took the opportunity to write some of these, leaving them with Reception for posting.

Wednesday 20th October

We all set off from the hotel on foot the next morning, after most of thc group had had an early breakfast, and followed a footpath through the woods, passing close to a stream where women were washing their pots. It was hot and humid and as the path led uphill, we noticed the luxuriant growth of the vegetation, where thickets of bamboo had stems like tree trunks, up to a foot in diameter.

"This area is noted for its heavy rainfall and mild climate," remarked Yin Hao. "The warm dampness causes problems for the hotel because towels go mouldy within a few days if they are not washed."

Further up, we crossed the stream and noticed a strong smell of sewage. We thought about the women washing up downstream and hoped that the hotel staff had somewhere more salubrious to clean their crockery. It was a misty morning but the rain held off. We soon reached some paved terraces where we stopped.

"This is a Buddhist monks' crematorium," Yin Hao told us. "It is a very sacred place. We will climb to the top terrace first."

At the top of the steps, we came to a broad platform, surrounded by lush bamboos and with three identical buildings on the far side.

"These are the furnaces where the bodies are burned," Yin Hao explained.

The furnaces were each about eight feet high and wide but only a couple of feet deep, with faded red walls and white concrete roofs. A red angled wall on either side of each furnace was capped in white stone with a green bamboo decoration, across the top of which undulated white stone dragons. A white goose-like stone bird perched at either end of the main roof while a white vase with a single flower stood in the centre, in front of the white brick chimney. Below this was the five foot high opening to the furnace over which was a smoke-blackened sign in Chinese characters.

After looking around, we descended the steps to the lower terrace where a high wall, also in faded red, was divided horizontally into five sections by rows of yellow tiles.

Each section had a series of recesses in which to place the ashes before the opening was sealed with a wooden door. There were both sealed and empty recesses at all levels right across the wall and a few wooden coverings stood on the ground, ready for use. The wall was capped in white stone with a green bamboo decoration, similar to that on the furnace roofs, while a pair of very long, white stone dragons undulated towards each other along the top of the wall.

In front of the wall stood a double row of sturdy stone monuments, each about twelve feet high, looking a little like giant chess pieces. Each of those nearest the wall had an upright tombstone in front of it and had been decorated with carvings of flowers and dragons. Some bore carved likenesses of the monks they were commemorating while others displayed a photograph of the deceased. Only one of the stone monuments in the front row had a tombstone and as yet, the stones remained shaped but uncarved. Descending the steps to the next level, we came to a terrace outside a Buddhist temple.

"This is where the monks practise kung-fu," said Austin. "I thought this would be the ideal place for a group photograph."

Nobody had any objection to this so while Austin sat on the ground, the rest of us arranged ourselves in three rows behind him with the tallest at the back and those in the front row kneeling. While we posed, Yin Hao obliged by taking photographs with everyone's camera in turn.

We then returned to the hotel and went by coach part of the way up Mount Emei, to a car park at Jingshui at a height of about eight hundred metres.

"The route to the top of the mountain is twenty seven miles long," Austin told us. "We will only be able to see a small part of it but it will give you an idea of what the climb is like."

From the parking area, we followed a paved path and steps which took us six hundred feet or so higher up the mountain. On the way, we passed a sedan chair park, the sedan chairs being stacked on one side of the path and looking like old-fashioned folding wooden deckchairs. These sedan chairs consisted of two long lengths of thick bamboo joined by four cross-bars. Attached to the two in the centre was a length of cloth, padded at one end, that sagged to provide a seat.

As we climbed, we saw porters conveying numerous visitors down the mountain but not a single person was being transported uphill. A middle aged Japanese man beamed at us and waved as he was carried past, thoroughly enjoying the experience. The sedan chair bearers ran along the paths and down the steps with their heavy loads. We found their sure-footedness quite amazing as the steps were of varying heights and unevenly spaced.

We were making our way six hundred feet further up the mountain to Wunnian Temple and although that may not sound very high, it took us about two hours to reach the temple and involved climbing many hundreds of steps. Having eaten nothing at all for thirty six hours, I found this quite exhausting and was grateful for the walking stick that had been given to David the previous afternoon.

On our climb, we passed what we thought was a school, a substantial two-storey building that seemed to be completely isolated in the forest. Children of varying ages were out in the stony playground where there were two table tennis tables, each supported by six piles of bricks. Two boys were playing at each table, surrounded by onlookers. They were hitting and returning the ball at speed, smashing it back and forth, and appeared to be skilful players.

Buddhist Crematorium

Mount Emei

Mount Emei

While I paused for a brief rest, we looked at the map. No school was indicated on the mountainside and there was certainly no village nearby.

"I wonder if it's a boarding school," said David.

"I don't know whether they have boarding schools in China," I replied. "Perhaps it's a holiday home." Because we were right at the back of the group and Austin, Li Mei and Yin Hao were all up near the front, there was nobody to ask.

After many more steps, we eventually reached Wunnian Temple, or Ten Thousand Years Temple, where the rest of the group were waiting for us. In a clearing in front of the temple, men were forcing monkeys to balance on one leg, holding a stick behind their heads while a large crowd stood around clapping their appreciation. The men were beating the animals to make them perform.

"It's sick," said Mattie, looking distressed.

"There's nothing you can do about it," said Austin. "It's part of the Chinese way of life."

Assistants were walking round collecting money but we were careful not to encourage them in any way and tried to ignore what was happening.

Now that David and I had joined the group, we moved across to a paved area beside the steps leading up to the temple's entrance gate, an impressive building with a three tiered roof. Here we stood while Yin Hao told us that the temple dated back to the ninth century.

"Wunnian Temple is still used as a monastery to this day" he said. "It is dedicated to a Bodhisattva named Puxian who is the symbol of virtue and the protector of the mountain. He rides in a golden lotus flower, on the back of an elephant with three enormous tusks on each side of its trunk. His statue in the temple is made of bronze and is eight and a half metres high."

Yin Hao then indicated a plaque on the wall. "This plaque tells the history of the monastery."

The beautiful reflecting background was in mother of pearl, while the history was printed in horizontal lines of Chinese characters in white, blue and gold.

"We are now going for lunch," he said. "You will have time to look round the monastery afterwards."

We followed Yin Hao into the temple complex and round to a large hall, set out with rows of long trestle tables with wooden benches on either side. Yin Hao led us to the far side of the room where a table had been reserved for our group. Although I was determined to starve for forty eight hours to ensure that I was rid of whatever bugs I had picked up, I sat with the others to be sociable. The monastery was vegetarian and the food looked very appetising.

"This is good," said David, helping himself from various dishes.

"You should try it," urged Jane. "This is the best meal we've had so far."

"I'm not hungry," I told her. "I'm quite happy with just a bottle of water."

"You really ought to have some plain rice," Austin said to me and John. "It's good for stomach upsets and it will give you some energy."

Although John was also not hungry, he put two small spoonfuls of rice in his bowl and ate very slowly. He was a little annoyed, after the meal, to be charged the price for a full set lunch. Austin had a word with Yin Hao, who spoke to the monk serving us and explained how little John had eaten, but to no avail.

"I'm sorry," Austin said apologetically, "but if you have eaten anything at all, you must pay the full price." Although the monks wanted to charge me the full price as well, I had had nothing but water so that was all I had to pay for.

"You are now free to do whatever you want for the next hour," Austin said, "but please be back at the entrance to the monastery at two o'clock."

"I'd like to climb higher up the mountain," said Adrian, one of the single men in the group. "Is anyone else coming?"

"We'll come with you," said Josh and Mattie. Several others decided to join them and they set off enthusiastically.

I had very little energy left so David and I stayed to explore the grounds of the temple and monastery. There was a large rectangular pool with a wall round it, edged with reeds and rushes and with a few water lily leaves in the centre. Yin Hao had told us that this pool was famous for its musical frogs, but we must have been there at the wrong time of the year or perhaps the wrong time of the day.

"I'd like to see the statue of Puxian," I said.

"I'll find out where it is," volunteered David. He found a monk who spoke English and asked him.

"It's in the Elephant Pavilion," he told us, directing us to a square brick building with a dome, tucked away in a corner and almost hidden by trees and shrubs. To get there, we followed a stone-flagged path between hedges and then climbed two short flights of steps.

Inside, we found that the base of the dome was painted with a ring of small Buddhas, while attached to the sloping roof of the dome were six shelves, each full of small Buddha statues. Around the pavilion at eye level were twenty two statues of Bodhisattvas, each behind a glass screen over which people were dropping money to have their prayers answered.

However, taking pride of place in the centre of the Pavilion was the magnificent bronze statue of Puxian, seated on a golden lotus flower on the back of a white elephant. Towering to a height of nearly twenty eight feet, it was most impressive. We felt it had been well worth the effort of the climb to see this.

We left the Pavilion and as we wandered round the temple grounds, we came to another pool surrounded by a white stone wall, on the inside of which were paintings of scenery, flowers and people.

"Look," I said to David, "each of those paintings has a different style and composition."

"Maybe the monks were told the general theme to be painted but each one decided for himself how it should look," he suggested.

"Perhaps they had a competition to choose the best," I said, deciding which one I would nominate as the winner.

While we were inside one of the temple buildings and David was trying to communicate with one of the monks, the monastery bells rang. The monk stopped what he was doing, banged on his drum with a large padded drumstick, sounded his gong and began to chant prayers. As we watched, he then took a spoonful of rice from a container on the temple altar and carried it to an offertory pillar outside in the courtyard. Here, he scattered the rice and chanted more prayers. This done, he was free to smile and attempt to communicate with us again.

He found a red envelope and pen and wrote a message in two vertical lines of Chinese characters which he presented to David with a little bow and another smile. David smiled in return as he accepted the envelope and thanked the monk. Later, he asked Li Mei what the monk had written.

"He says that you are a very nice, friendly person," she translated. "He says he is honoured to have you visit the temple and thanks you for taking such an interest." David, in turn, felt honoured and put the envelope away for safekeeping.

When the group met up at the temple gate, those who had climbed further up the mountain came back seething with anger.

"There were some more men with monkeys up there," Mattie complained. "They were forcing them to smoke cigarettes while a crowd of Chinese stood around clapping and laughing."

"The Chinese seem to think that animals have no feelings and are simply there to be exploited," grumbled Liz.

"It made me feel ill to see them," groaned Jess.

Austin let them finish protesting and then told us that we had a choice of two routes back to the coach.

"I shall be taking the more interesting route but it involves a further climb, which is followed by quite a steep descent," he said. "If you'd like to come with me, I'll lead the way. The other route is actually slightly longer but is a very gentle, scenic way back to the coach park. If you go that way, you can't get lost."

He added, "You'll have plenty of time, whichever route you choose. Just make sure you're back at the coach by four o'clock."

David and I chose the scenic route as I had little energy to climb further up the mountain. The steps took us beside a river that ran down a series of waterfalls through the forest.

We stopped to talk to a young Chinese woman, carrying her toddler daughter on her back in a beautifully made wicker basket. This had raised sides, with a padded seat for the child and a lower compartment for her legs and feet, and was fastened with leather straps over the mother's shoulders and round her waist.

We came to a place where the river flowed through a gorge and around a small island on which stood a pavilion, its roof turning up at the corners. On either side of the pavilion, a bridge curved steeply over the river. Mandy, who was with us, went into raptures.

"That looks so picturesque," she enthused. "You go on without me. I'm going to have to stop and make a sketch."

Further down the mountain, the gorge came to an end. The path broadened out and we came to some stalls displaying a variety of herbs, fungi and spices. We had reached a high level plateau and two rope bridges took us across the river that had now widened and was again divided by an island.

Although the water was shallow here, it was still flowing swiftly but the bridges looked well maintained and we felt quite safe as we crossed them. There were wooden planks to walk on and a waist-high rope handhold on either side so we enjoyed the bouncing, swaying movement.

The path now brought us to some farms near the track and we realised we were close to the car park.

"I'd rather not get back too early," said David. "Have you got enough energy to try one of the side paths?" We had reached a signpost indicating the direction to the Middle Peak Temple.

"Give me five minutes to rest and we'll go exploring," I said.

We found that the route to the Middle Peak Temple was up a rough, unpaved footpath where the only other person we met looked like a farmer. He was very friendly and spoke to us in Chinese, enunciating each word very slowly, clearly and loudly, at the same time writing the Chinese symbol on his hand to ensure that we could comprehend what he was saying. It was so like the old-fashioned stereotype of an Englishman shouting at a foreigner to make himself understood that I found it difficult not to laugh.

We ran out of time before reaching the temple and on the way back down, met a teacher who could speak some English. He was also returning to the car park and as we tried to communicate, it seemed no time at all before we were back at the coach.

From the mountain, we were all taken to the hotel and once back in our bedroom, I began to feel hungry. We had finished the chocolate but in our luggage, we had some shortbread that we had brought from home in case of emergencies. I decided to have a small finger of this to see whether I could keep it down. I felt much better after I had eaten it but wanted nothing more that day, other than water.

In the evening, the group went out to eat. The road near our hotel was lined with Sichuan Hot Pot restaurants and as we walked up the hill, young girls outside each one called out what sounded like "Savannah."

"That is the local dialect for 'come and eat'," said Yin Hao. He took us into one of these restaurants where raw food was cut very thinly and piled up on plates to be cooked by the diners in spicy boiling water.

Although I was not eating, I found it quite entertaining watching the others in the group choosing their pieces of food, which mainly consisted of vegetables, picking them up in their chopsticks, cooking them in the water and then eating them. It was a very slow, leisurely way of eating and passed the evening very pleasantly.

Thursday 21st October

The next morning, as I had suffered no ill effects from the piece of shortbread I had eaten the previous evening, I joined the rest of the group for "Western Breakfast". We were each given a plate on which were arranged two soft dough rolls with butter and jam, a hot hard boiled egg in its shell, a few cold potato chips, two slices of banana, a slice of raw tomato and some raw cabbage. The rolls, butter and jam were delicious but I did not attempt anything else.

We had packed our cases and after the meal, left all the luggage with the hotel Reception to be taken to Emei station. It was a very grey, misty morning but at least it was dry as we set off in the coach.

"'Sichuan' means 'Four Rivers'," Yin Hao told us. "We are now going to Leshan to see the Giant Buddha, which sits at the confluence of two of these, the Min and the Dadu."

As we were being driven through an area of farmland, he told us, "A wide, flat plain stretches from Emei to Chengdu, where you will be staying tonight. This plain is very fertile and known as the Land of Plenty. Since they have been allowed to own their own land, peasants in this area have become very rich and some are factory owners, despite the fact that they are not educated and are unable to write their own names."

He added, "The biggest black Stock Market in the world thrived in this area for many years and many fortunes were made."

"And no doubt lost," murmured Gordon, who was sitting behind us.

"The Government now controls the Stock Market," continued Yin Hao, "and there are no longer such large profits."

The scenery was not that interesting and we were pleased when Yin Hao broke the journey for us to visit a pot-making factory. Unlike the light, friable soil near Cheng Gong, the ground here was made up of heavy yellow-brown clay. We climbed out of the coach and watched as three men loaded lumps of this clay into wheelbarrows.

They brought it over to the open shelters that made up the factory, close to where we were standing, emptied out the barrows and started to tread the clay, kneading it by walking up and down on it while it squelched beneath their bare feet. "A bit like treading the grapes," grinned Alan.

When it was considered sufficiently kneaded, the clay was taken to a wooden table in one of the shelters, where the master potter used a wooden rolling pin to roll it out like pastry. When he decided it was thin enough, the flattened clay was wrapped round the sides of flowerpot-shaped moulds, cut to shape and left to dry until it reached a consistency where it could be removed from the mould without losing its shape. Under the shelter were two or three hundred of these new bottomless clay pots, standing in rows, continuing to dry out. We supposed that the base of each pot was added later.

Now that we had seen the pot-making process, Austin proposed that we should take another walk through the fields and we followed a very muddy path beside a river, where a water buffalo stood in the water and a woman crouched down on the opposite bank, doing her washing. The fields were divided up into rectangular shallow lakes, where young rice was growing and white ducks were foraging for food between the plants.

"Rice is a popular crop in this area as the clay holds the water," said Yin Hao, as he left the river path. The lakes were separated by very narrow, muddy footpaths and we kept slipping as we balanced our way along these.

There were only a few women working in these fields but those that we saw were most concerned about the mud plastering our shoes. The women were all barefoot, which seemed very sensible.

One woman, standing in the water, put her hand solicitously on my shoulder and said something to me, in Chinese. It was very clear from her gestures that she was telling me to be careful not to fall.

It was hard work trying to stay on the narrow raised strips and we were thankful when Austin led us towards the edge of the field where the ground was higher. As we slithered and squelched up the muddy steps cut into the clay, we did not envy these farmers one little bit.

We went a short way along a path which led uphill into a forest, passing a woman who was leading her water buffalo by a rope round its neck. This woman was wearing boots. As she saw us, she stopped to let us go by with smiles and 'ni haus' and her buffalo took the opportunity to feast on the lush greenery growing beside the path.

As we made our way back towards the coach, this time on the higher path, we saw a man using his water buffalo to plough his rice field, which was perhaps fifty feet long by twenty feet wide. The buffalo was harnessed to a small wooden plough, the man following behind through the muddy water with his trousers rolled up above his knees.

"Are snakes a problem?" wondered David.

"There are snakes but not that many," said Austin. "Most of them are caught and eaten."

We had been walking for about an hour by the time we were back at the coach and we wiped as much mud as possible off our shoes before boarding. As we continued on our way to Leshan, Yin Hao told us that this was once the provincial capital.

"As I mentioned before, Leshan is situated at the confluence of the Dadu and Min rivers," he said. "Although it is not far from Emei, the local dialect is so different that people from the two towns are unable to understand each other."

This seemed strange when these communities were only separated by a flat plain but the rivers would have made formidable barriers.

Leshan was a prosperous-looking market town with tree-lined streets. Once the coach was parked, Austin said, “We’re going for lunch first but bring with you everything you’re likely to need for the afternoon.”

He led us to a tourist restaurant and we climbed the stairs to the first floor, where we discovered that the building backed on to a road running beside the river.

We were shown to our two tables and Li Mei placed the order for our meal. We were the only ones in the restaurant and looking around, David spotted a door leading on to a balcony.

“Let’s have a look at the river,” he suggested. While we were waiting for the food to arrive, several of us went outside. The cloud was low and the river was almost invisible through the mist.

“Phew, what’s that smell?” asked Josh, wrinkling his nose. Anna looked over the end of the balcony.

“It’s coming from here,” she said. A steady stream of ripe smelling sewage was running down the wall from the public conveniences on the floor above. We did not stay out there for long.

After lunch, Austin told us, “I’ve arranged for a pleasure steamer to take us across the Min River to see the Giant Buddha. It should be waiting opposite the restaurant.”

We walked over to the river but there was no sign of the steamer. “Stay here,” said Austin. “I’ll find out what’s happened to it.”

He went off to make enquiries and when he came back, he told us, “Apparently, our boat has been commandeered for a tour of the Yangtse. Give us a few minutes and Yin Hao and I will try to make other arrangements."

He and Yin Hao walked along the river bank to talk to other boat owners and between them, they managed to hire another craft to take us across the river. While Austin came back for us, the owner put a gangplank over to the bank so that we could board.

This boat had folding metal seats on deck and sat so low in the water that it looked as though the addition of any further weight would cause it to capsize. Austin realised the danger and as we crossed the gangplank to the boat, he directed us to either side of the deck and asked us to spread ourselves out along the full length of the vessel.

"When we get close enough to see the Buddha, please don't all rush to one side," he warned us. "Take it in turns and change places one at a time."

We set off and as we chugged along at a snail's pace, little wavelets splashed on to the deck. Further from shore, we found that where the rivers converged, we were passing hidden rocks and shoals and skirting mini waterfalls and whirlpools. The water was actually flowing at several different levels and we seriously wondered whether we would make it safely across. Once through the danger area, we moved a little faster and eventually, through the mist, we could make out the head and neck of the Buddha, which were a light grey against the darker rocky cliff.

As we drew closer, we could see the Buddha's lower legs, his enormous fingers resting on huge stocky knees. On either side of the seated Buddha was a niche containing another statue carved from the cliff face.

These side statues, possibly of guardians, were also huge but they only reached to the height of the Buddha's knees.

There was nowhere to bring the boat in to shore as the cliffs fell almost vertically to the river, with a raised platform above us round the feet of the Buddha. We landed further up the river to find the coach waiting.

As we crossed the Min River by bridge, Austin explained, "I wanted you to take the river trip first, because that's the only way to see the entire carving of the Giant Buddha."

In the coach, we headed back towards the statue and then took a winding road up the cliff, as Yin Hao told us the story of how the Giant Buddha came to be constructed.

"At the beginning of the eighth century, many boatmen were killed by the treacherous currents where the two rivers, the Min and the Dadu, converge," he began. "A monk named Haitong decided to carve a huge Buddha in the cliff face overlooking the confluence, in the hope that he would calm the waters and protect the boatmen. This monk organised all the fund raising himself and hired the workers to carry out his project. At the monastery above the Giant Buddha, there are two statues of Haitong, who is revered by the local people."

"This massive undertaking took three generations to complete and the construction of the Giant Buddha actually achieved its purpose," Yin Hao went on. "During the carving, excess rock was dropped into the river, filling the deepest parts of the river bed which made the crossing safer." He added, "This Buddha is the largest in the world. He is seventy one metres high and even his big toe is more than eight metres long."

The coach stopped in a parking lot and Austin said, "First, we're going to walk up to Li Win Monastery at the top of the cliff. 'Li Win' means 'above the clouds' and the monastery is now a museum. You'll have a chance to see more of the Buddha afterwards. When we reach the monastery, I must ask you all to keep together as a group through the temple area, as it gets very busy."

Inside the temple was a room of Buddhas and a collection of Bodhisattvas which were quite entertaining to see. Several were making the most fearsome grimaces and one had enormous eyebrows that grew down below his shoulders. These Bodhisattvas, like others we had seen, were protected by glass screens over which people could throw their money in the hope of having their prayers answered. There was also a hall with a thousand small statues of monks, every one of them different.

After going round the museum, Yin Hao allowed us an hour to climb down the statue to the Giant Buddha's feet and back up again, should we wish to do so. Nearly all of us decided to go. The descent started by the grey head of the statue, whose ears alone were seven metres long. Even though we were very close to the statue, it was still difficult to comprehend its enormous size. The Buddha was beginning to succumb to Nature and although his head and shoulders were clear of weeds, greenery was sprouting from elsewhere, particularly along his arms and legs. However, considering the age of the statue, it was in a remarkable state of preservation.

The steps down were very steep, zigzagging out towards the river and in towards the cliff. Below us, tiny figures were walking around the feet of the Buddha. As we were going down a section looking across at the river, David said, "Wait. I feel really dizzy."

"Stop a moment, hold on to the handrail and look at the cliff opposite," I suggested.

I too could feel the effects of vertigo. The river seemed to pull me and I had a sensation of falling towards the water. After a few minutes I asked, "How are you feeling? Do you want to go back up again?"

"No, I shall be all right if I take my time," said David, ready to continue the descent.

All the way down the rock face on either side were cavities of varying sizes, the reddish colour of the rock indicating that it was soft sandstone. The steps followed down the Buddha's right side and there were some recesses near the base of the statue which were probably more sheltered from the elements, as they still contained the remains of statues carved out of the rock.

All the other niches appeared to be empty and some were quite eroded. From here, we were unable to see the very large guardian statues on either side that we had observed from the water.

At the base of the statue, David rested for a while on the end of one of the Giant Buddha's toenails, recovering from the descent. He was relieved to be down.

I felt fine as soon as I reached the bottom of the steps. I stood at the railings overlooking the river to watch a cruise ship motor by, its bow shaped like the head of a dragon, with a curling tail at the stern. Near the Buddha's feet, several photographers were waiting for customers to dress up and have their commemorative pictures taken.

It was now time for the return climb. On the far side of the Buddha, David and I found an unlit tunnel through the rock and when we explored, found that although it was very dark, it was quite short and led to a much gentler route back up the cliff face. As usual, the enterprising Chinese had set up their stalls wherever the path was sufficiently wide and were selling wall hangings covered in Chinese characters, fans, model Buddhas and numerous other souvenir items to tempt visitors.

At first, the path wound gently round the cliff, with steps taking us first a short way up and then down again. The river views would have been wonderful on a clear day. Further round, the path was cut into steps and began climbing more steeply.

The narrow steps and path had been carved out of the overhanging cliff face and the very low wall on the outer side would have done nothing to prevent us going over the edge. Luckily, the path was surrounded by vegetation that hid the drop below us and gave a false sense of security. Once we reached the top, we had an amazing view of the route by which we had descended the cliff.

We spent some time here and had a drink at a café before making our way to a white stone pagoda. A queue of people waited for tickets to climb the stairs to a viewpoint at the top.

"Do you want to go up?" I asked.

"No," decided David. "It's so misty, there's not much point. In any case, we haven't time to queue. We have to be back in ten minutes." We returned to the coach where the rest of the group were already waiting.

Shortly after we set off for Emei, Austin told us, "It's time for our next factory visit, guys. We're going to see a silk carpet factory."

The coach parked at the front of an old brick building and we were shown into a single room, bare of furniture apart from the looms. These stood along the right wall of the room, furthest from the windows, with a bench in front for the women who were working on the partly finished carpets.

We learned that the silk was delivered in tangled skeins which first had to be unravelled and wound into balls. The balls of different coloured silks were then hung beside the looms and the carpet weavers cut off the lengths required with a metal blade before knotting the silk by hand. The patterns were worked from memory with no visible guidance as to how the finished article should look.

Once a carpet was completed, it was passed to the checkers, women who stayed close to the windows where the light was better. They sat either on the bare concrete floor or on that part of the carpet they had already checked, with the section they were working on over their knees. It was their job to spot any errors in the pattern, unpick the mistakes and fill in the resulting gaps with the correct colours.

After we had watched the women at work, we were taken through to the showroom where they hoped we would purchase some of their rugs and carpets. These were very expensive and we were not popular when we pointed out several flaws that the checkers had missed.

Back in Emei, we went to a restaurant at five o'clock for our evening meal where, among other dishes, we were served fish with spam – an unusual combination.

Giant Buddha of Leshan

Mao statue, Chengdu

Chengdu panda

School party

During the meal, we said our farewells to Yin Hao, who had been a good guide. We then left for the station with Austin and Li Mei to take the six o'clock train to Chengdu.

Austin took us to the left luggage area and said, "We haven't much time. Find your bags as quickly as you can and follow me." Luckily, he had already collected the tickets in advance and had ascertained where the train would be waiting.

We had to hurry with our cases past all fifteen carriages of the train that was standing at the platform, before climbing down on to the tracks and crossing several lines to another train. Austin and Li Mei confirmed it was the one we wanted and then, once they had identified our carriage, we had to get on board. As we were down at track level, this was easier said than done.

Austin and Phil climbed on first and we passed them our bags, which they quickly stacked on the shelves provided at the end of the carriage. It was then our turn to clamber on to the train.

The bottom step was more than three feet above the tracks and we had to use the handrails on either side to pull ourselves up. Luckily, we were all wearing loose fitting trousers. It would have been an impossible feat in tight jeans.

Julie and Jane, being shorter than the rest of us, both needed a helping hand from above but we were soon all aboard and found our seats with only minutes to spare before the whistle blew and we were on our way.

7

Chengdu

It was midnight by the time the train pulled into the station at Chengdu. As we were being driven to the Grand Hotel where we were spending the night, Austin told us, "Chengdu is the capital of Sichuan Province and is also known as Brocade City."

The place had a big city atmosphere but on arriving at the hotel, we found that, despite the fact that it boasted five Chinese stars, it looked slightly shabby. However, our room was comfortable enough and we wasted no time getting to bed.

Friday 22nd October

We had to be up early to pack our cases and take them down to Reception where they were stored in a small room behind the desk. We then went through to the restaurant for breakfast.

At this hotel, we were given a breakfast menu and Gordon was excited to see that porridge was one of the items on offer.

"I love porridge," he said, ordering it.

Joanne was doubtful. "I don't think it will be made from oats," she said.

Austin had a knowing look on his face but said nothing. When the porridge arrived, much to Gordon's disgust, it turned out to be a bowl of watery ground rice.

At eight o'clock, we met our new local guide, Susie, another very young, pretty girl with long black hair. As we set off in the coach, she said, "I hope you all like pandas. This morning, we're going to visit Chengdu Zoo, which has the biggest panda collection in the world. I'll be taking you straight to the panda enclosure."

Our visit coincided with that of several school groups and when we arrived, we found about sixty children, all aged between eight and ten, leaning over the wall on one side of the panda enclosure.

"At the present time, the zoo has thirteen pandas," said Susie. "They are housed in six cages which are all connected to this exercise area. We will stop here for a few minutes to give you a chance to see them."

We spread out around the enclosure for a better view. We were looking down into a large circular pit which had a concrete path about four feet wide running beside the vertical outer wall. In the centre of the enclosure was a raised mound with a flat grassy top on which stood a climbing frame. The sides of the mound were of steeply sloping concrete studded with cobblestones, presumably to provide a grip.

Two of the pandas put in an appearance and wandered along the path round the enclosure, so everyone had a good view of them. They were large, cuddly looking creatures with thick white fur and contrasting black ears, smudged black eye patches and black limbs, the colouring of their front legs extending to meet above their shoulders. However, even from about ten feet above them, looking over the parapet, we could see the long claws on their massive paws.

One of the pandas lay on its back, reclining against the stony central mound, one paw raised as though it was waving to us all. The other decided to crouch with its head down. The children all began yelling something at the same time and the sound was deafening. I put my hands over my ears and grinned at an elderly man standing nearby.

"What are they shouting?" David asked him.

"They are saying, 'Stand up, bear,'" he replied.

Somebody threw some food down into the enclosure and the panda that had been lying on its back rolled forward on to its feet and went over to investigate. The noise erupted again as all the excited children yelled their approval.

After a few minutes, Susie on the far side of the enclosure waved to us and we all made our way back to her. "I hope you enjoyed the pandas," she said. "Before we leave the zoo, I want to show you a different type of panda, the red panda."

She led us to another enclosure a short distance away. It was constructed in the same way as the first enclosure but walking around the perimeter path were four animals that reminded me of raccoons.

They were about the size of a very large cat with fur the red-brown colour of a fox, dark brown legs and thick bushy tails with lighter red-brown stripes. Their face masks were very distinctive with white edgings to their ears, white eye patches, white cheeks and snouts but with a contrasting black line of fur running round the top of the snout and a black button of a nose. They looked rather endearing.

As we made our way back through the zoo to the coach, we passed crowds of young school children, all waving to us and shouting, "Hallo, goodbye." They became so excited when we waved back and replied.

After seeing the pandas, it seemed only natural to visit a bamboo factory. When we arrived, Susie took us inside and explained that bamboo was one of the wonder products of China.

"It is used extensively in building and provides sturdy uprights, strong but light roof beams, roof tiles and pipe work," she said. "It is also used for food and here, in this factory, it is split down into threads no thicker than that of coarse cotton, and is woven into trays, plates, bags and boxes."

The bamboo threads had been dyed many different shades and we watched the women at work, weaving them together to create a variety of goods in all kinds of colours, patterns and shapes.

We then went round the shop where we discovered that bamboo had also been used to provide woven covers for ceramic vases and tea services. Some of the designs were over-fussy for my taste but there was one tea service I rather liked.

The teapot was covered in a light beige bamboo with a ring of chequered black and white round the top of the teapot above the handle and spout. The matching Western-style cups had a similar band of black and white running through the upper part of the handle, about an inch from the rim. There were also matching handle-less Chinese-style mugs, the black and white band running round the upper part of the mug and the edge of the matching lid. The tea service stood on a matching tray. However, I felt that they were for display rather than practical use.

Vases, ranging in size from about two to eighteen inches high, came in a variety of shapes. Their woven bamboo covers were patterned in geometric stripes, squares, diamonds and circles and some had scenes sketched on plain backgrounds which must have been painted on once the weaving had been completed. Handbags, boxes and other small items also came in a variety of sizes, shapes, colours and designs.

This was the only factory we visited where we were tempted to buy and the goods were reasonably priced. David and I purchased a Mah-Jong set made of black and white bamboo spliced together and two packs of carved bamboo chopsticks. I then spotted a little woven circular box with a white background patterned with red, gold and green and a panda painted on the inside of the lid. “That would make an ideal gift for Sarah”, I said, thinking of one of our friends. David agreed and we added it to our purchases.

As we were being driven back to Chengdu in the coach, Susie giggled and said, “It’s always cloudy in this part of Sichuan. If the sun comes out, it’s so unusual that the dogs all bark and cower in fear.”

She added, “The city is prosperous and was one of the first places where people were allowed to sell goods on the free market.”

“Does anyone own their own house?” asked John.

“A few people can buy their own property but most live in company flats,” she replied. “A factory worker would start in a one-room flat but if they stayed with the same company for more than twenty years, they would be able to work up to a two-room, possibly a three-room flat. Some really good companies provide flats with up to five rooms but employees who manage to get one of these would only use two rooms regularly and would keep the others for guests."

Back at the hotel, we had half an hour to spare before lunch. There was a park opposite and David and I decided to take the opportunity to look around. We went through the entrance gate and discovered that concrete paths, edged with bamboos, led to a series of open spaces, each with a central flower display.

One had a large shrub on a raised area in the middle of the display, on top of which stood a large cockerel in red and gold, with black and gold wings and a tail that appeared to be made from real feathers. The shrub was encircled by a raised tier of yellow chrysanthemums from which segments of yellow, mauve and white chrysanthemums radiated out to the edge of the circular bedding area. All the plants grew in pots, so it would have been very quick and easy to completely change the design of the park.

In another square was an artificial hill with two gently sloping grassed ramps, the centre of each bearing the design of a flying bird outlined in small pink bedding begonias. The top and bottom of the hill were again covered in pots of chrysanthemums in contrasting colours.

While we watched, two teachers organised a class of young children into three rows in front of the flying bird design, girls on the right and boys on the left in height order. Those in the front row went down on one knee and while one teacher stood behind the children, the other took a photograph of them.

The girls all wore red jackets and although the boys were dressed in a mixture of colours, each had a red kerchief knotted round his neck. This group of thirty children were aged about eight and had probably come to the park from the zoo.

As we walked round, we came across many other groups of children who all shouted “Hallo, goodbye” to us. We had a few postcards of England which we had thought might make good presents and David made the mistake of throwing these out among one group of children. They squabbled over them and we were then surrounded by about a hundred children who followed us through the park, hoping for more postcards. “I feel a bit like the Pied Piper,” said David.

We waved to the kids as we escaped from the park and made our way back to the hotel where we were meeting to go to lunch. Much to our surprise, Susie then took us back to the park, where there was a restaurant.

Over the meal, Susie told us, “When I was at school in the mid-1980s, there were eighteen classes for each age group, each with about fifty children. Now, with the birth restrictions, at that same school there are only five classes of forty children for each age group.” It brought home to us how recently China had adopted its single child policy.

After eating, we had a further hour to explore Chengdu by ourselves. David and I decided to walk to the statue of Mao, which marked the city centre.

On the way, we passed an expensive looking restaurant. The extended roof canopy was supported by a double row of red pillars with golden dragons twisting round them. Over the entrance hung festoons of fairy lights and on either side of the door stood a large vase of brightly coloured plastic flowers. Two young ladies in full length blue satin gowns waited to welcome customers for lunch.

The statue of Mao stood on a pedestal at the top of a long flight of steps, one arm extended as if in benediction. Despite the fact that he was responsible for China's Cultural Revolution, bringing misery and hardship to many and destroying much of the country's ancient heritage, Mao was still apparently held in high regard and his statue had a place of honour in most cities.

Several bicycles had been left propped up at the foot of the steps. Bicycle theft was clearly not a problem in Chengdu. We climbed the steps to the statue, behind which stood a four storey concrete building that turned out to be the Exhibition Hall.

At the top of the steps, we looked back at the main street below. Between the wide pavements, a dual carriageway in each direction for motorised traffic was flanked on either side by an even wider cyclists' lane. It was a busy time of day and all parts of the road were crowded, although traffic was moving freely.

Although it was not raining, the sky was heavy and overcast. The scene looked grey and misty but it was brightened by gaudy advertisement hoardings attached to the roofs of the buildings opposite. At regular intervals down our side of the street, colourful balloons each floated high on the end of a broad white ribbon with red characters down its length and narrow white banners with red characters hung across the full width of the road.

We looked in some of the nearby stores and in the window of a china shop displaying porcelain dinner and tea services, I saw some lovely Chinese tea mugs with lids. I had been hoping to purchase a couple of these as an attractive and useful souvenir of China and these were in a beautiful design and colour. David liked them as well, so we went into the store and made enquiries.

One of the assistants took us to the manageress who spoke good English. I explained what I wanted.

"I'm very sorry," she said, "but we cannot sell you two separate mugs."

"Does that mean we would have to buy a set of six if we want them?" I asked.

"No, we could not do that either," she said apologetically. "They are part of a service and you would have to purchase sixty pieces, which includes all the dishes and the soup tureens."

That was the end of that idea.

We also went round a department store where we were surrounded by assistants trying to serve us. Susie told us afterwards that the Government guarantees everyone a job.

"The main department store in Chengdu has more than two thousand sales assistants," she said. "Although most of them have nothing to do, it gives them more pride than living on benefits."

As we walked back towards the park and hotel, I saw some items for sale on a stall and could not make out what they were. A young student, seeing us looking at them, came over and explained that they were peeled citrus fruits. He asked permission to talk to us for a few minutes to practise his English and told us his name.

"Does that have any special meaning?" I asked him.

"It means 'From the Forest'," he replied.

"My name is David, which means 'Beloved'," David told him.

This obviously made an impression because when he left us, the student said to David, "Farewell, Beloved, you are beloved by the people of China and must return often," which we thought was charming.

As we passed another restaurant, I was puzzled by a man in the street. In one hand he was holding a plucked duck and in the other, a burning newspaper which he was waving under the duck.

"Surely he isn't trying to cook it," I said to David.

David asked a passer-by who told us that the man was a cook and was singeing the hairs off the duck. He said it in a tone of voice that indicated we should have known this, because it is always done in the street over burning newspaper.

Back at the hotel, we collected our luggage and boarded the coach which took us to the airport. Here, we said our farewells to Susie, who had been another good guide.

As we walked across the tarmac towards our China Northwest aeroplane for the flight to Xian, in Shaanxi Province to the north, I was surprised to see that the windows along the side of the aircraft were all below wing level and pointed this out to David. I do not recall ever seeing this before or since, but it seemed a good idea as it allowed for uninterrupted views.

The flight was over spectacular mountain ranges, the mountains very jagged with narrow ridges that appeared to be only a few feet below us. I was lucky enough to have a window seat and while I was enjoying the panorama, the air hostesses came along with drinks and packets of sweets and nuts for us all.

"That wouldn't be allowed at home," I said, looking at a packet of Dar'kie peppermints, picturing the white face of a smiling minstrel singer dressed in a black and red striped top hat and dickey bow, his black lips open to reveal a set of impossibly white teeth.

David had been looking at the ingredients listed on the back of one of his packets of sweets. "Look at this," he said, grinning.

In English it read, "This product is specially refined from pure Chinese natural herbs, luhankuo, prune, peak fog tea, peppermint with functions to provide you to have total refreshment, particularly helpful for smoothing oral cavity, lowering body hot, eliminating bad breath and against thirsty. It gives you a sweet scented feeling with pleasant taste."

"They'll do you good," I laughed. Then I looked at my packet of Amber Walnut Kernels.

"Look," I said, "these are even better for you."

The back of this pack informed us that "The refined amber walnut kernel manufactured and developed by our factory has unique flavour and is excellent in colour and taste. It has many magic functions; increase intelligence and invigorate brain; moisten lungs and remove phlegm; smooth skin; make trichomadesis regrow; turn white beard black; beautify face; invigorate blood circulation and strengthen bones; prolong life. It is the perfect food for travel and as a gift to relatives and friends."

"Do you think 'make trichomadesis regrow' means that it's a cure for baldness?" laughed David.

"I reckon so," I grinned. "These walnut kernels can do anything."

"We ought to buy up all the packs available in China and sell them to the medical and beauty professionals in England," chuckled David. "We'd soon be multi-millionaires."

It all added to the enjoyment of the flight, even if none of us looked noticeably younger or healthier as we left the aircraft in Xian.

8

Xian

Shaanxi Province

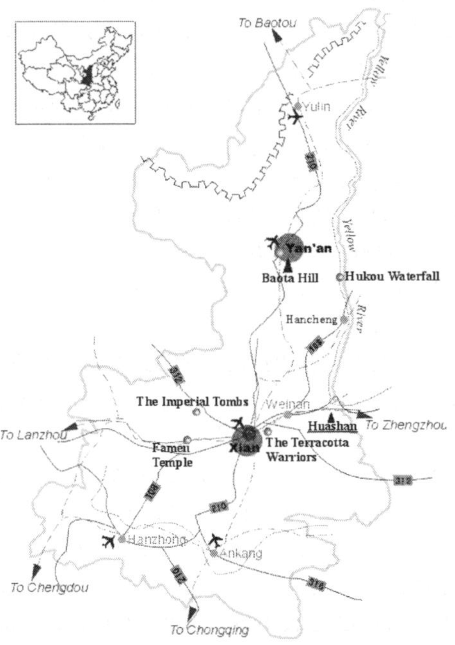

Because Xian was her home town, Li Mei was allowed to combine her role of national guide with that of local guide while we were here. As we were waiting for our luggage to be unloaded, she told David and me, "For the first time since the beginning of the tour, I will have an opportunity to see my husband this evening."

"Do you have a child?" I asked.

"Not yet," she said. "We have only been married a few months."

"What does your husband do?" enquired David.

"He is the company secretary for a large tobacco company."

On the way from the airport, Li Mei told us all that Xian was the capital of Shaanxi Province and was one of the most historical places in China.

"People have been living in this area for more than six thousand years, since prehistoric times," she said. "In the third century BC, China was unified into a single state under Emperor Qin Shihuang who had his capital close to where Xian now stands. This Emperor believed in immortality and spent much of his lifetime creating a city within a tomb, guarded by armies of Terracotta Warriors. You will learn more about this when we visit the site tomorrow."

"During the time of the Qin and Han Dynasties, about two thousand years ago, the Chinese empire was expanding," she went on. "The capital was moved a short distance to the site of present day Xian in the sixth century AD, during the Tang Dynasty. It became one of the greatest cities in the ancient world, rivalling Rome and Constantinople in importance. It covered an area of eighty square kilometres and was surrounded by a wall more than five metres high. Because the city was built on a flat plain, it was comparatively easy to defend. Any enemies first had to cross the mountains to reach the plain and, if they managed that successfully, they could then be seen approaching from a distance."

We drove through modern Xian and came to a high wall surrounding the historic centre. As we passed through a gate, Li Mei told us, "Everything you will want to see in Xian will be within these walls. Unlike the original city walls, these enclose an area of less than twenty square kilometres and it is very easy to find your way around, as the roads are arranged in a grid system. If you get lost, you should ask for directions to the Bell Tower, which is close to our hotel."

We were driving round a large building when Li Mei pointed it out. "That's the Bell Tower," she said. "It was first built in 1384 during the Ming Dynasty. There are large bronze bells inside that were once rung to tell the time. In 1739, the tower was moved to its present position in the city centre where two main roads cross. In Xian, it is forbidden to build anything higher than the top of the Bell Tower."

We had now arrived at the City Hotel where we were staying, right in the heart of the old city. While we were waiting for our room keys, Austin gave us each a map of that part of Xian within the city walls, showing our hotel highlighted in red.

We were given a short time to take our luggage up to our rooms and freshen up and then, shortly before five o'clock, met up for our evening meal in the hotel restaurant.

That night, the food was delicious with slightly thicker soup than usual, made with sweetcorn and egg, and real meat with no bones. Amazing! We were very pleased because Harry and Lucille were celebrating their forty fourth wedding anniversary.

Harry had told us, earlier in the trip, "Lucille comes from Belgium. I was a pilot with the RAF when we met during the war. She was just a teenager at the time but we stayed in touch, met up again and married a few years later." It was all very romantic.

Austin had found out about the wedding anniversary and we had clubbed together to buy them a large bottle of champagne and a card. They asked the hotel staff for glasses and shared out the champagne between us all. Alan had composed an amusing poem in their honour which he read out, making them laugh, before we all drank a toast to the still devoted couple. It made the evening very special.

After the celebrations, David and I went out to have a closer look at the Bell Tower. Each side of the square base was approximately a hundred and twenty feet long with an archway in the centre. On top of the high walls of the base stood a square building, four storeys high, each storey having decorative red columns and a green curving roof. A simple gold ornament took pride of place in the centre of the top roof.

A young couple came over to talk to us, so David asked if the Bell Tower was the oldest building in the city.

"I do not know but I think the Bell Tower is not so old," the young woman said. "Perhaps about three hundred years."

We discovered that the couple lived in an apartment outside the city walls and had only been married a short time. They had come into the city centre to see a show. After chatting for a few moments, they had to leave and we went to explore further.

A short way down one of the main roads, we discovered the local cinema and peeped inside. It was absolutely packed. I saw some posters outside and said to David, "Look at this. You can hire your own private box."

A photograph showed customers sitting in a row of boxes watching a film. One long box had been partitioned off into several single seat compartments, each with its own door at the front. Each compartment was probably about two feet wide, high enough at the rear to provide a backrest and a little lower at the front, so the seated customer could see the film over the door.

"I wonder whether there are two seater compartments for courting couples," grinned David.

"There aren't any shown but I'm sure they could squeeze into a single box," I said.

We wandered a little further down the street before David decided, "I'm feeling tired. Let's head back to the hotel. We can explore another day."

We made our way back to the City Hotel and our comfortable room, where we relaxed and enjoyed some green tea before going to bed.

Saturday 23rd October

When we awoke, the sun was shining. This was the first actual sunshine we had seen since the Guilin river trip at the start of our holiday and the way it lifted our spirits was amazing.

"I like this place," said David happily.

When we went down to the dining room, we found that at this hotel, Western breakfast really was. There was toast, the first we had seen since we left Hong Kong, plus butter and jam, fresh orange juice, scrambled eggs and ham. Wonderful!

That morning, Li Mei took us to see the Terracotta Warriors. On the way, she explained to us, "Emperor Qin Shihuang came to the throne at the young age of thirteen in 246 BC. During his reign, the Qin conquered four separate states and the Emperor standardised the currency, language and script of the five formerly independent countries to make a single nation."

"However," she went on, "the Emperor was obsessed with immortality and throughout his lifetime, he was making preparations for his death. His tomb is known to be inside a hill. It has not been excavated but is reputed to contain palaces and pavilions full of treasure, with trees made from precious stones and rivers of mercury. The ceiling is said to be inlaid with jewels to represent the sun, moon and stars. However, the tomb is protected by various devices and traps to kill anyonc who attempts to break in. When the Emperor was buried, all his slaves, wives and concubines and all those who had worked on the construction of the tomb were buried alive with him to keep its details secret."

"The outer wall of the mausoleum is said to be six kilometres long and is protected by vast armies of terracotta warriors," she continued. "Nobody knows how far these armies extend. In 1974, a group of farmers were digging a well, one and a half kilometres away from where the edge of the tomb lies buried, when they uncovered the statue of a warrior. When excavations were carried out, they discovered eleven long pits containing thousands of warriors and horses in battle formation. Archers with crossbows and longbows were at the front, followed by soldiers with spears and axes. Soldiers on the end rows faced outwards to defend against any enemies attacking from the sides. In this one vault alone, there were six thousand figures plus thirty five horse-drawn chariots. The excavations are now covered and protected by an exhibition hall. We shall visit this first."

"Two further vaults were discovered in 1976," she added, "and since then, a vault of female warriors has also been found. You will discover more when we go round the museum afterwards."

Our coach was one of many and people were queuing to view the warriors. There were signs all round the exhibition hall indicating that photographs were forbidden.

"Don't attempt to take photographs of the figures," Li Mei warned us. "There are guards everywhere and your camera will be confiscated. You can buy postcards in the shop afterwards."

Once inside the building, we climbed steps to the viewing platform and looked down on the rows of warriors. The hall was like an enormous warehouse with small windows all round to let in some light but the place was so large that we could hardly see to the far end.

The warrior statues were lined up in columns separated by thick earthen walls as high as the warriors' shoulders. They stood three or four abreast and each cohort of about fifty men was followed by four horses. There was then a space before the next cohort began. This was possibly where a chariot had once stood but I was unable to see any chariots. Many warriors had an arm extended forward, indicating that it had once held a weapon.

When we had had a few minutes to take in this amazing sight, we were moved on by the guards to allow room for the next contingent. Li Mei was waiting for us outside.

"The warriors were originally painted and you will be able to see how they differ from each other when we go into the museum," she told us. "They all have differently shaped faces, different hairstyles and expressions and differently shaped moustaches and beards."

The museum was a fascinating place. There were examples of the warriors so that we could see from close up the amount of detail that had gone into their construction. Most had long hair, knotted at the back or on top of their heads in varying styles, while some wore hats. The majority sported beards and moustaches but whilst one had a pencil-thin moustache along his upper lip and a little tuft of beard in the centre of his chin, another had a long upturned handlebar moustache with a point of beard on either side of his chin and a third had a short bushy moustache with a short beard stretching from ear to ear.

All appeared to be dressed in thick winter clothing with long sleeves, kilts and boots but the armour covering their upper body and shoulders differed in design and some wore high-collared coats under their armour, while others seemed to be wearing scarves. Most were standing, their hands curled round weapons that had rotted away over time, but a few, probably archers, were down on one knee. All were beautifully crafted.

In the museum, we learnt that the warriors in Pit Number 3 were all facing inwards rather than outwards and that there were more generals, these being shorter and stockier than the other warriors and wearing a different uniform. This was thought to be the army HQ that controlled the other armies.

A separate building housed smaller than life-size bronze chariots and horses, my favourite part of the exhibition. The bronze animals were far more detailed than those in terracotta and still wore their harnesses. The leading charioteer stood in a two-wheeled backless carriage under a large circular parasol/umbrella holding the reins of his four steeds. He carried bronze swords, a spear and arrows in a quiver on his back and in his chariot were a crossbow and bronze shields.

Behind him, a further four horses pulled a low, enclosed two wheeled carriage with a small window on either side and a seat at the front for the charioteer, who was armed with a spear.

"This carriage would have been a replica of the one the Emperor used while alive and was intended to transport his spirit after death," Li Mei told us.

Both chariots were originally decorated on the outside with gold and silver and were made up of over three thousand different parts, welded together. Photographs of the inside of the Emperor's carriage showed that this, too, was decorated in intricate patterns of gold and silver. It was all fascinating and when Austin indicated that it was time to go, I was reluctant to leave.

Just outside the site was a market. "I've had a look round here before and this is a very good place to buy your souvenirs," Austin suggested. "You have half an hour here but please be back at the coach by twelve o'clock."

"I wouldn't mind having a silk dressing gown with a dragon on it," said David.

"Let's have a quick look at them all first to see what's available," I suggested.

After walking round several stalls, he stopped in front of one that mostly stocked children's clothes but had a few adult dressing gowns in blue and black with magnificent dragons on them

"I'd like that one," he decided, pointing it out to the stallholder. The one he had chosen was in black silk lined with white silk and embroidered with golden dragons on the back, either side of the front and down the sleeves. The stallholder fetched it down from the rail and David made sure it was large enough for him.

"How much does this cost?" he asked.

"One hundred and thirty FECs."

"You must be joking," said David sounding shocked. "I'll give you ten FECs." He eventually bargained the price down to sixty FECs and the stall holder still seemed reasonably pleased.

"I'll wrap it up for you," he said. He went round to the back of the stall with the dressing gown and emerged with a parcel. David unwrapped it before leaving, to find he had been given a cotton unlined dressing gown.

"This is not the one we agreed on," he said and went round the back of the stall himself to find the silk dressing gown.

"There is no need to wrap it," he said and as he had paid the negotiated price, the stall holder had to let him take it. "Well, he didn't have to accept my offer if he thought it was too low," reasoned David.

Some of the others in our group then tried their luck and Phil managed to purchase an unlined silk dressing gown for the same price as David's but nobody else did as well as he.

From the market, Li Mei took us to a restaurant where we had an excellent lunch. As one dish arrived, Julie said excitedly, "Those look like potatoes." She tried one and found it had a coating of caramel. "Yes! Toffee potatoes," she cried.

Having been deprived of potato for so long, we had all developed a yearning for them. Although there was only sufficient for a tiny piece each, they tasted wonderful. I never knew I would miss the humble potato so much. There was also a bowl of persimmons, sufficient for one each. These looked like large rotten tomatoes but the fruit inside was delicious.

After lunch, we went by coach to Huaqing Hot Springs. "There has been a Royal palace beside the hot springs for about three thousand years," Li Mei informed us on the way there. "It was extended in the third century BC, during the Qin Dynasty, when a stone pool was built and it was enlarged again during the Han and Tang Dynasties."

"The Tang Emperor, Xuanzong, used the palace as his winter resort because the hot springs prevented the lake from freezing over and warmed the surrounding air," she continued. "This is where he brought his favourite concubine, Lady Yang, said to be one of the most beautiful women in China and it is said that he was so enchanted by her that he neglected his duties as Emperor, resulting in a rebellion against him."

Bell Tower, Xian

Bargaining

Huaqing Hot Springs

Street scene, Xian

"The hot spring water remains at a constant temperature of 55° Celsius and is funnelled through a series of public bathhouses," Li Mei added. "There are also several larger pools. The mineral water is said to be very good for the skin. If you would like to try the baths, there are individual bathrooms and it is possible to hire a towel."

When we arrived, Austin told us that we had half an hour before we had to be back at the coach.

"If you want to go into the baths, I'll show you where to join the queue. There should be just enough time if you're quick."

"Do you want to go in?" I asked David.

"No, it would be too much of a rush and I'd rather see the place," he said. I felt the same way.

Mattie and Josh decided to bathe in the hot springs and Austin went with them to buy the tickets. The rest of us followed Li Mei who told us that the pavilions were rebuilt in 1955.

"The Dowager Empress Cixi took refuge here, after Allied Forces captured Beijing at the start of the twentieth century, but Huaqing is now used as a health resort," she said. "There are hospitals and convalescent homes within the complex. Mao's wife used to come here every year to bathe and take the waters."

The setting was very pleasant, with a wooded hillside rising up behind the main lake, known as Nine Dragon Pool.

"The mountain is called Lishan and is more than one thousand two hundred metres high," Li Mei informed us. "'Li' means 'black horse' and from a distance, the shape of the mountain resembles that of a galloping horse. On the slopes, there's a temple dedicated to Nu-

Wa, mother of the human race. Chiang Kai Shek took refuge here and in 1936, he was hiding in a pavilion on the mountain when he was arrested, because he allowed the Japanese to overrun China while he ignored them, preferring to fight against the Communist Red Army."

David and I then wandered round by ourselves and found a marble dragon boat. One of the pavilions had a curved terrace and round the base of its wall, jutting out over the waters of the lake, was a series of dragon heads, the dragons all with their mouths wide open.

"I like those," I said. "Do you think they were for drainage?"

"Maybe," agreed David, "or perhaps, at one time, they were fountains."

Further round the lake, we discovered the source of the spring which was in a filthy-looking well with a thick scum on top. "I hope the water is filtered before it reaches the baths," said David, wrinkling his nose.

At the foot of the hill we came across a wall, steps and circular gateway which looked interesting, but there was no time to explore further. We only had a few minutes to spare when we left Huaqing to return to the coach.

Just outside the entrance was a market and we went to have a very quick look at what was on offer. Most of the stalls at this end of the market belonged to fur traders and their furs still had the heads and tails attached. A salesman tried to put one of the furs across my shoulders and could not understand why I did not want a dead animal round my neck.

Further on, close to where the coach was parked, all the stall holders were selling silk dressing gowns. As well as being folded in their wrappings on the stalls, these hung in three or four tiers from ropes and from metal rails. They were made from both silk and cotton, lined and unlined, mostly in black, red and royal blue and covered in embroidery. Many had bands of embroidery round the neck, cuffs and hem and down the front but the most popular design on the blue and black garments seemed to be either embroidered or appliquéd golden dragons.

As we were looking at these, we met Jenny and Martin. “Do you want to try bartering for a silk dressing gown for me?” asked Martin. David had obviously acquired a reputation for getting a good price.

While Martin was choosing one, we were joined by John who said, “I wouldn’t mind one of those.”

David and John had fun trying to bargain the prices down but were not that successful. They had banded together and were trying to buy two dressing gowns together at a cheaper price when Austin called us to board the coach.

“We’ll have to leave it,” decided Martin and walked off towards the coach.

“Sorry,” David said to the traders, “but we have to go.” One of the stallholders followed us and was still desperately trying to bargain with John through the coach window as we pulled away.

From Huaqing, we went to see the Neolithic Village at Banpo, to the east of Xian, close to the Chan River.

“This is the oldest known agricultural village in China,” Li Mei informed us. “It is thought to have been occupied about six thousand years ago, at the end of the Stone Age.”

She told us that in 1953, the foundations of forty six houses were unearthed, the earliest houses being at a lower level than later ones. An exhibition hall had been built over the remains of the residential part of the village and this was where we began our visit.

There was also a museum of tools and pottery found on the site. As we went round the hall and museum, we learned how these Stone Age people had lived.

The oldest houses, with a floor level about a metre lower than the present ground level, came in two designs, circular and square. Each building was constructed from four uprights, attached to which were walls of pliable interwoven branches covered with a mixture of clay and straw. Both designs had steep thatched roofs and the square design also had an entrance tunnel facing south, the end of which would have been sealed with a woven door. Each house had a fire pit and both fire and steam were used for cooking.

Some of the later huts were on stilts, with openings for light and air and even internal walls to separate different rooms. The mud walls and floors would have been lined with wood. Considering that this was the Stone Age, they seemed to us remarkably advanced in design.

The residential part of the village was surrounded by a moat, about two metres deep and two metres wide, which would have helped to protect the village from wild animals and would also have acted as a drainage ditch. On the far side of the moat were the pottery kilns and the burial ground.

"When a child died, it was buried upright in a pottery urn, close to the house, to keep the child's spirit close to the family," Li Mei informed us. Adults were buried with their possessions in wooden caskets in the cemetery and among the articles found were ornaments such as bone hairpins and beads made of stones, shells, bones and teeth. There were bone needles and fish hooks while tools included stone axes, knives, arrowheads and millstones.

The people used bows and arrows for hunting and caught fish with harpoons and nets. They grew crops and used hemp and rattan for spinning and weaving. Their pottery was decorated with colour, geometric patterns and designs of scenery, fish and animals and the lids for the pots were sculpted into artistic shapes. Pots of water were used to keep food fresh in the summer, through evaporation.

These Neolithic people even used a rudimentary form of writing that formed the basis for the earliest Chinese characters. David and I came away feeling awed and convinced that these people were far more advanced than others around the world at that time.

That evening, back at the hotel, we had another excellent evening meal. Afterwards, David and I wandered down to the South Gate, one of twelve gates in the wall and the closest one to our hotel. It was nearly dark when we arrived but it looked interesting so we decided to return the next day.

Sunday 24th October

We had a free day to explore Xian on our own. The morning was misty but dry and after breakfast, David and I set off for the South Gate again. In front of the gate and to the right of it, a long, decorative and very large dragon, that looked as though it may have been used for Chinese New Year processions, rested along the roofs of a row of single storey wooden buildings. To the left, another gateway led us into an area of the old city that had a character all of its own.

The wide paved road had a slightly raised pavement on either side but there was no traffic, other than a few bicycles, and people were walking down the middle of the road. Gleaming yellow litter bins with blue legs and blue lids were spaced at intervals along the pavement and everywhere was spotlessly clean.

The buildings on either side were three storeys high, the ground floor being used as a shop or restaurant with living accommodation on the two floors above. Most of the shops and restaurants had red paper lanterns hanging outside and the shopkeepers clearly took a pride in keeping their premises looking smart and attractive. Even the few street vendors were using good quality tables for selling their wares, rather than the cheap trestle tables we had seen elsewhere, and everything looked upmarket.

As we walked down the street, we saw a number of people wandering into a courtyard.

"Let's see where they're going," suggested David.

We followed them and discovered a complex of old, picturesque buildings around the open square. These had overhanging bamboo tiled roofs supported on red pillars, between which were beautifully decorated wooden friezes. The overhangs provided covered walkways outside the buildings, which had low brick walls topped by decorative screens of bamboo and glass.

A young man came over dressed in dark casual trousers, a jacket with rolled up sleeves and a plain bright red T-shirt.

"Can I help you?" he asked.

"We were wondering what this place is," I said.

"You are now in the music and art college of Xian," he said, introducing himself with a little bow of the head. "I am one of the teachers here. Please, permit me to show you around."

How could we resist?

We started in the music school where he took us to some of the classrooms. Although it was Sunday, one or two of these held a solitary student practising on the piano. They must have been aware of our presence but we were ignored completely.

From there, we went to the art school. The teacher took us into a room where water-colour paintings and ink drawings hung side by side, covering almost the entire wall. Each piece of art was mounted on an attractive sheet of backing paper with a brocade-like design, mostly in gold on blue or in blue on gold, although there were other colours.

Attached to the top was a wooden batten with a string, while the bottom was fastened round a shiny black lacquered wooden bar, that weighted the artwork so it hung correctly and was also used to roll it up for transport. We admired the paintings which had much more character and individuality than those we had seen in the shops and factory outlets.

"All these paintings are for sale," said our guide. "You just tell me which ones you like and I will tell you the price." There were so many wonderful designs, many of which we liked, that it was difficult to choose.

Eventually we selected a watercolour of an old man teaching his grandchild how to use an abacus. The faces of the man and child were most expressive and we knew that it was a painting we would enjoy for many years. The backing sheet was about three feet wide by about five feet long and we had no idea where we would find the space to hang it but we knew we would make room somewhere.

When we asked the price, we were shocked by the figure asked but the teacher was open to bargaining and in the end, we bought the painting for less than half the price originally quoted. The teacher then rolled it up for us, tied it with the top string and placed it inside a long cardboard container covered with the same brocade design as the backing of the painting. One end of this container slotted into the other. The container was then, in turn, carefully wrapped in brown paper and tied with string.

With David clutching our purchase, we made our way further down the street and found some steps leading on to the city wall.

"We ought to walk on the wall," I said.

We climbed the steps and discovered that, unlike the comparatively narrow walls of English mediaeval cities such as York or Chester, this city wall was a vast affair. It was nearly forty feet high and also nearly forty feet wide, paved in a light coloured stone and with a parapet on either side. At intervals, there were defensive towers and steps down to the city and the wall stretched as far as we could see, vanishing into the mist in the distance.

"Which way would you like to go?" asked David.

"We'd better have a look at the map," I said.

There were stone seats along one side of the wall and we sat on one of these to look at the plan of the inner city.

"There's a Taoist temple near the East Gate," suggested David. "We've been walking in that direction so it can't be too far away."

"Sounds all right to me," I agreed and we set off along the wall.

Wc had only gone a short distance when a man came across and started chatting to us. He asked where we were going and when we told him, offered to show us the way although we assured him that this was not necessary.

He insisted that he wanted to practise his English with us and began by asking general questions about where we came from and how we liked China. After about five minutes, he started suggesting that we should change money with him.

"I'm collecting foreign exchange certificates to be able to travel abroad one day," he told us. "I will give you a very good rate of renminbi in exchange."

Wanting to be helpful, we offered to change a ten FEC note, worth just over £1.00, since we thought that even if he gave us out-of-date currency, it would make little difference to us.

"We don't have many FECs left," said David. "This is all we can spare."

The man then started trying to persuade us to go to a bank to change travellers cheques for more FECs. We refused, saying we had already bought all the souvenirs we needed and did not want to have too many renminbi as we would be unable to change them back at the end of our holiday. At this he went quite huffy.

"I have better things to do than to talk to you," he said, "but without me to show you the way, you'll get lost."

He hesitated, giving us an opportunity to change our minds, but I said, “Don’t worry, we have a map.” He left in disgust and we were glad when he was gone.

We were then befriended by a group of five young Chinese visitors, two men and three women, who spoke no English. They indicated their map to ask where we were going but we could not see the Taoist temple so we showed them where it was on our copy of the map. They smiled and nodded and then accompanied us, chatting to each other in Chinese.

It took us about half an hour to walk to the corner of the south and east walls where there was a watchtower. The walls covered a total distance of fourteen kilometres and although we estimated that we would be walking only about three of these, it still seemed a long way. It took us another twenty minutes to reach the East Gate but here we found a barrier built across the wall and no way down.

We and our five Chinese friends had to walk back to the south wall before we could descend to street level. They then guided us through the city to the East Gate and we bowed and said “xie xie” several times, expecting them to leave us to do their own sightseeing. To our surprise, they conferred briefly before indicating that they would be taking us all the way to the temple.

We left the main road and walked miles round a maze of back streets, our Chinese friends continually asking the street vendors for directions. We were feeling very tired and our guides were also obviously wilting but determined to complete their mission.

Having finished all our water on the wall, by this time we were also very thirsty. We mimed that we would like to buy them a drink, thinking that we could all have a rest at the same time. However, they refused to pause or give up until they eventually brought us to the temple entrance, where they bowed and prepared to leave us.

We again suggested that they might like a drink with us but they declined. Li Mei had told us that 'dor xie' meant 'thank you very much' so we bowed to our new friends and said 'dor xie' several times but it seemed so inadequate for all their time and effort in helping complete strangers.

"The first thing I need to do is have a rest," I said. David walked over to the temple steps.

"We can sit down here for a few minutes," he said, taking the weight off his feet. I quickly joined him.

After a short time, we had regained enough energy to explore. The temple turned out to be well worth the visit. It had a beautifully decorated bell-tower with rows of good luck figures striding down each corner of the roof.

In front of a long stone container, holding burning candles and joss sticks, was a low bench covered with woven and embroidered kneeling mats which we had not seen anywhere else. There were also many different musical instruments arranged on the altar inside the temple.

Just outside the grounds, stall holders were selling paper money for sacrificing to the ancestors. Opposite the temple was a street of calligraphy with a fine ornate gateway at the far end.

"That looks interesting and we might find a café or restaurant down there," I suggested.

We walked down this street and found shops selling paintings as well as examples of calligraphy and sign writing. However, there was still nowhere to buy water or any other drink and the people we asked were unable to assist us. We had packed lunches provided by the hotel but we were getting desperate for liquid refreshment.

"I suggest we go back to the hotel for our lunch," said David. "At least we can make a hot drink and sit down to eat."

"Good idea," I agreed. "Let's see if we can find a taxi."

Through the gateway at the end of the street, we found a line of motorcycle rickshaws. Each motorcycle had a two-wheeled two-seater carriage attached on the back, a flimsy material-covered framework protecting the top, back and sides.

David went up to the first one and negotiated a price to take us to the Bell Tower. Once this was agreed, we climbed on board. The seat had been designed for smaller Chinese bodies, but we somehow managed to squeeze in together and our driver started the engine and set off, clearly determined to get us to our destination as quickly as possible.

We had a most exciting, nerve-racking ride through the back streets of Xian, weaving in and out between stalls and traffic at breakneck speed and with several very near misses. We were relieved to arrive safely without hitting anything or anybody and as David paid the driver, I felt my legs shaking.

By the time we were back in our room, it was about three o'clock so we were ready for lunch. The hotel had provided two large Chinese mugs with lids and some sachets of green tea so, while David checked whether the boxed painting would fit in his suitcase, I opened two of the sachets and found that they contained large leaves which I put into the mugs, before pouring on the nearly boiling water from the urn. The lid of the mug proved useful for holding back the floating leaves but it meant that two hands were required to drink the tea.

I sat back in one of the chairs and sipped with a sigh of satisfaction. "That's what I needed."

"We'll have to carry the painting separately," said David, leaving it on the bed. "It's too long for the case." He took his own mug of tea and sat down.

We then opened our lunch packs but found the food very dry. I enjoyed a hard boiled egg but there were several pastry items with tiny amounts of filling. David found one with something a little like dry spicy mincemeat in it but we found the other items too stodgy so we left them.

Having had a hot drink, something to eat and a rest, we were now feeling much better.

"Are you ready to see some more of Xian?" I asked.

"Let's go towards the West Gate this time," suggested David.

We left the hotel and made our way to the Bell Tower and from there to the Drum Tower. This looked like a smaller version of the Bell Tower except that it was rectangular in shape with a long roof ridge. A young man came up to us, gave a little bow and asked permission to tell us about the Drum Tower.

"I am a student and would like to practise my English," he said.

"What do you know about the tower?" I asked.

"It was first built in the fourteenth century during the Ming Dynasty and inside, there are drums that were once beaten to tell the time," he told us. "It also marks the beginning of the Muslim quarter of Xian. Would you like me to take you to the Great Mosque?"

"Yes, please," said David. "That sounds interesting."

Our guide beamed. "Follow me," he said. He led us down some back streets and paused outside one of the buildings.

"First, you should have a look at this art exhibition," he suggested. "The paintings are very good and you can buy them. I will leave you here for a while," and he hurried away.

"He's obviously being paid to find potential customers and bring them here," I said.

"I don't mind looking at some more paintings," said David. "We can find the mosque later."

We went inside and enjoyed looking at the artwork on display. Although the majority of the paintings were the traditional ones we had seen many times before, there were also some more unusual ones.

"I do like that one of the Silk Road," David said.

"I haven't seen them all yet," I protested.

However, having had a time to view the other paintings, we both came back to that particular one. It was a water colour showing a fort on the side of a mountain and to my mind, the scene looked Tibetan. There was no detail to it but the outlines painted with a few strokes of the brush were so skilfully done that they stimulated the imagination.

"Let's buy that one," I agreed.

After a great deal of hard bargaining, we eventually reduced the price to an amount we were prepared to pay and had another lovely souvenir. As before, the painting was rolled up from the bottom, tied with its hanging cord and placed in a long brocade-patterned box where one end slid inside the other to fit the width of the painting. This was then wrapped in brown paper and tied with string.

Thrilled with our purchase, we then found our own way to the Great Mosque by asking directions. We were expecting to see Arab domes and minarets but instead found a building that looked like another Chinese temple. However, there was Arabic lettering outside the Prayer Hall, which we were not allowed to enter.

There was little time to explore further as an early meal had been arranged for the group at our hotel that evening. After eating, we were taken by coach to see the Tang Dynasty Show at another hotel.

At the start of the show, the compère informed the audience in several languages that in the seventh century AD, during the Tang Dynasty, Chang'An, the former name of Xian, became the largest city in Asia and one of the largest in the world.

"Chang'An had a million inhabitants within the city walls and a further million outside," he announced. "It was an international trading city with a thriving religion and culture. The dances we are putting on for your entertainment this evening are authentic reproductions of the Tang dances of Chang'An, based upon pottery paintings and descriptions by writers from that time."

The dancing was beautifully choreographed and there were some lovely costumes. Between the dances, music was played on traditional instruments which included small drums and a large ornamental drum on a stand; a double row of bells; gongs; wind instruments similar to flutes and oboes; and a large variety of string instruments, some played with a bow like a violin, some plucked like a guitar, while long instruments lay along the floor with one end supported on a cushion.

It was difficult to believe in the authenticity of the dances when one, which was supposed to show peasants celebrating a good harvest, was danced by young men twirling around in tights and leaping about like ballet dancers. However, perhaps this was a genuine seventh century dance, as performed for the Emperor and his court, to represent the joy of the peasant farmers.

There was a lovely graceful dance where girls, dressed in robes in rainbow colours, spun great lengths of material around themselves in wide loops and swirls. A similar dance was later performed by nine girls wearing full length, white embroidered dresses with sleeves about four feet long, that they twirled into patterns as they moved. All the girls had long hair piled high on their heads in elaborate styles and decorated with large silk flowers or jewelled headdresses, depending on the dance.

As usual, the performance lasted precisely seventy five minutes and provided us with a very enjoyable and entertaining evening.

Monday 25th October

The next day, we had to pack our cases early and bring them down to the lobby before breakfast. While we had our meal, the luggage was loaded into the coach which was waiting outside and as soon as we were all ready to leave, we set off to visit the Big Wild Goose Pagoda. On the way there in the coach, Austin told us the legend.

"One winter," he began, "the meat-eating monks that lived in the pagoda were starving and one of them came out to search for food. A flock of geese flew overhead and the lead goose, sensing the monk's desperation, sacrificed itself and dropped dead at the monk's feet."

As the story unfolded, we found out that unfortunately, this sacrifice was rather wasted because the monks were so overwhelmed by the selflessness of the goose that they promptly turned vegetarian, buried the goose with full honours and named the temple after it.

Li Mei then told us the real history of the temple. "The Big Wild Goose Pagoda was built in the seventh century by a Tang Dynasty Emperor, in honour of his mother who had died," she said. "It was used to protect the first Buddhist scriptures to be brought back from India and translated into Chinese. During the fifteenth century, the temple was rebuilt and additional floors were added. At one time, there were ten storeys altogether but the upper floors were later destroyed during an earthquake."

"When we arrive, you'll have time to climb the pagoda to see the view," she added. "There are nearly seven hundred steps to the top. The Tang Emperor's poetry is on the walls, so people can read it as they climb the stairs."

Austin put in, "Every brick in the pagoda had the mark of the maker on it so if any was faulty, the Emperor knew who was responsible. This was an early form of quality control."

As we laughed, he added, "When we arrive, you'll be free to wander round by yourselves. The pagoda is an important Buddhist temple but you might also like to have a look at the side pavilions. One of these is dedicated to Chairman Mao and the walls are decorated with Mao badges."

The coach park was below the pagoda and to get to it, we first had to walk through a souvenir shop. This was stocked with some very attractive ethnic items but, as usual near the tourist sites, they were very expensive.

The Big Wild Goose Pagoda was square in shape, its seven storeys getting progressively smaller towards the top. The outside was very plain, the only decoration being a built-in column effect in the cream brick walls and a double row of patterned bricks in the same colour under the eaves on each floor. The brown bamboo roofs were short and straight with no upturned corners, although as we approached, there appeared to be some good luck figures along the edge of the very top roof and hanging from the corners of the lower roofs.

When we reached the pagoda, the outside of the ground floor looked more colourful, the covered walkway round the building being supported by red pillars and with parallel strips of predominantly blue patterned boarding attached to the ceiling. Panels of glass and bamboo in the walls let in the light but the design was still fairly basic.

This was reflected inside, where the temple was very plain compared to some we had seen. As it was another grey, misty day, we did not make the effort to climb the stairs to see the view.

Outside the temple stood a three-legged metal urn containing a smoking fire, where people were lighting candles and incense sticks and placing them on stands, where bamboo coverings kept off any rain.

Xian Art College

Xian City Wall

Big Wild Goose Pagoda

Hitching posts

Musician, Shaanxi Provincial Museum

We found the Mao pavilion where his statue, small and white, stood on a large red pedestal. Behind the statue were panels of Mao badges, in a variety of sizes and colours, arranged in patterns.

From the Big Wild Goose Pagoda, the coach took us to the Shaanxi Provincial Museum, noted for its steles. When we arrived, Li Mei first took us to a room filled with ancient tombstones and guardian statues, some well over two thousand years old. She gave us plenty of time to look around and then asked us to follow her.

"We are now going to visit seven rooms filled with stone tablets," she said. "These are collectively known as the 'Forest of Steles' and are the heaviest collection of books in the world. The earliest date back to the Han Dynasty, at the start of the second century BC, but they represent all periods of Chinese history up to the Qing Dynasty which ended in 1911."

As we entered the first stele room, we saw some large, upright, dark stone tablets, each about seven feet high and three feet wide. Chinese characters had been carved out of the polished stone and painted white, to show clearly against the dark background.

"In this first room," Li Mei told us, "there are thirteen classical books inscribed on one hundred and fourteen stone steles. They include a book on medicine, one on the history of China and another covering the teachings of Confucius. Students had to learn these books by repetition. Their knowledge was then tested in oral examinations."

As we went round the museum, we learned that the tablets in the second room were carved during the Tang Dynasty when Chinese calligraphy was said to be at its best. The third room held a calligraphy collection illustrating different writing styles.

"There are five varieties of script," Li Mei informed us. "These consist of seal characters, official script, regular script, running hand and cursive hand."

One writing style looked a little like shorthand and Li Mei told us that even the Chinese find it difficult to read.

"These writing styles are copied by students of calligraphy," she said. "Children in school learn the official style of writing used in printed books but artists and sign writers tend to copy various styles from the fifth, sixth and seventh centuries AD."

In one of the seven rooms, which between them housed about two thousand three hundred stone tablets, we saw what I thought of as the Chinese equivalent of brass rubbing taking place. One of the tablets was being patted with a black powder that looked like soot. A white sheet of paper was then placed over the tablet and smoothed against the stone with brushes so that when it was removed, the paper showed the engraved white calligraphy standing out against the black background. These sheets of paper were being sold in the shop.

When we went out into the grounds of the museum, we saw a large collection of weathered stone posts with worn carvings, each with a different decorative figure on top.

"What are these?" asked Anita.

"They are hitching posts where travellers once tied their horses," explained Li Mei.

We were attracted to a display of traditional instruments in another room by the sound of a young woman playing a lovely Chinese melody by plucking the strings of a horizontal string instrument that lay on a table. We went to listen but unfortunately, when she saw we were taking an interest, she started playing 'Auld Lang Syne' to please us. It was such a pity.

From the museum, we went for an early lunch before heading to the airport where we took a flight to Beijing. We were served a light meal on board and arrived in the early evening.

9

Beijing

Hebei Province

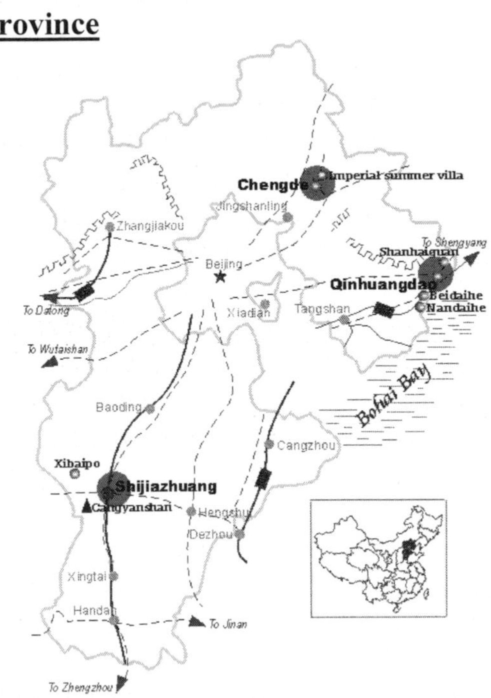

As we left the airport, we noticed a distinct chill in the air. We were met by our new local guide, a tall, broad shouldered young man in a red woollen jacket.

"My name is Charles," he said haughtily, looking down his nose at us. "Follow me to the coach."

My immediate impression was that he was an arrogant young man who had a very high opinion of himself and a very low opinion of foreign tourists. For some reason I could not put my finger on, I also felt he was a conman who could not be trusted.

We were driven straight to a restaurant for our evening meal, after which we were taken to our hotel in Beijing, the Tiantan. As we walked into the hotel, the heat hit us.

Austin grinned at our reaction and said, "I've found in Beijing that during the summer when it's hot, most hotels and restaurants use excessive air conditioning, so you need to put on extra clothing when you enter a building. Conversely, as soon as the temperature drops to freezing, the central heating is turned on at full blast. There seems to be no happy medium."

As he handed out the room keys, Austin said, "I shall be going on a city walk later on. If you'd like to join me, be back in the lobby in fifteen minutes."

He then passed each of us a map of the centre of Beijing showing our hotel, located between Tiantan Park and Longtan Park.

"I thought we could all walk together to Tiananmen Square," he said. "It will give you an idea of distances."

As we entered our bedroom, the heat felt even more stifling.

"Phew, it's like an oven in here," said David. "Can we open the window for a few minutes to let in some fresh air?" I went over to check.

"I'm sorry, it's locked and I can't open it," I said.

We looked for some way to alter the central heating but the hot air was blowing from a vent above the door and there was no temperature control in the room.

"We'll definitely go on the walk," said David. "It will be a relief to be out in the fresh air again."

While we were waiting in the lobby, we found Tiananmen Square on our map. It was about five centimetres from our hotel but there was no indication of scale. As soon as everyone had arrived, Austin set off at a fast pace.

After about twenty minutes, poor Harry, who was in his early eighties, was finding it hard to keep up. Lucille was quite concerned about him. David and I were near them at the back of the group so David hurried forward, had a word with Austin and asked him to slow down. Austin came back to Harry and Lucille.

"Are you all right?" he asked.

"Yes, I'm fine," said Harry, although he looked very pale.

"I'm sorry we were walking so quickly," Austin apologised. "I was up at the front with some of the younger members of the group and didn't realise there was a problem. I'll try to take it more slowly from now on but there is still quite a distance to go."

"I can manage," insisted Harry. "I want to see Tiananmen Square."

"I think we need to rest for a few minutes first," Lucille put in diplomatically. Austin considered.

"We'll be visiting the Forbidden City on Thursday and there'll be plenty of time to see Tiananmen Square then, so you won't be missing anything if you don't want to walk that far. Look, I'll show you where we are now on the map."

He pointed it out on his copy and Harry and Lucille confirmed the location on their own map.

"There's no need to stay with the group," Austin went on. "You can decide whether you want to continue to the Square at your own pace or whether you would rather return to the hotel. If you use the map, you can't get lost." Harry and Lucille thanked him and he went back to the front of the group to lead the way again.

"Will you be all right?" asked David, concerned, as everyone moved on again.

"Yes, thank you, we'll be fine," Lucille assured him. "You go on while we have a rest and decide whether to continue."

Harry was now looking much better and we left them there while we caught up with the others. It took about an hour before we finally arrived in Tiananmen Square and we were amazed at its vast size.

"Tiananmen means 'Gate of Heavenly Peace'," Austin told us. "Back in Mao's time, during the Cultural Revolution, there were parades of up to a million people here."

We had come into the Square at the south end and Austin pointed out Mao's Mausoleum.

"After your visit to the Forbidden City, you will probably have time to visit the Mausoleum if you want to," he suggested. "Also, if you are very keen, you could walk down here early one morning to see the flag raising ceremony that takes place at sunrise."

David looked sideways at me.

"I think we'll be giving that a miss," he grinned.

We walked with Austin to the north end of Tiananmen Square where there was a small garden in front of a high wall with a tall pavilion behind it. In the wall were five archways with a picture of Mao over the central one. The wall was floodlit in pink and green.

"That's Tiananmen, the Gate of Heavenly Peace that gives the square its name," Austin informed us. "It's the entrance to the Forbidden City. You may want to spend the rest of the evening around this area."

He pointed in the direction of the taxi ranks.

"You can get a taxi back to the hotel from over there. It's not very expensive. I shall have to leave you now as I need to get back to do some paperwork." He waved and hurried away.

"I could do with a drink before I go any further," said Joanne.

"If we walk down the road, there's sure to be a café not far away," suggested Gordon.

They went along the main street to the right of the Forbidden City and most of us went with them as there was nowhere in particular that we wanted to see. We had walked two blocks when we came to the Beijing Hotel, very Art Deco in style.

"This looks a nice place," said Julie. "I'm going in here to see if I can get a coffee." We all followed her inside and sat in comfortable armchairs in the lounge where we were served with cakes and cups of coffee.

We were resting and chatting when Josh said, "Mattie and I spotted a MacDonald's sign on the way here and decided we'd love some hot chips. Would anyone like to join us?"

As we thought about it, our mouths started watering. We had now finished our cakes and drinks so we left the hotel and made our way across to MacDonald's where we all ordered chips, David and I sharing a portion.

We were not usually fans of MacDonald's but it was wonderful to taste potato again, even if it was rather on the oily side. Afterwards, some of the group decided they were going to explore further but David and I had had enough for one evening and took a taxi back to the Tiantan Hotel.

Tuesday 26th October

After breakfast, Austin and Charles were waiting for us in the hotel lobby.

"I have to take time off this morning to confirm your flights home," said Austin, "so I'll leave you in the capable hands of Charles." As Austin made his way to the lifts, Charles immediately began to annoy us by clapping to get our attention.

"This morning we're going to visit the Summer Palace," he said. "Follow me to the coach."

On the way to the Summer Palace, Charles ignored us completely and talked to the driver in Chinese. When we arrived, he clapped at us and ordered, "Follow me and keep together." At the entrance, he bought the tickets and then clapped at us again and waved us to follow him.

Once inside the grounds, Charles told us, "During the Qing Dynasty in the seventeenth and eighteenth centuries, several Imperial Gardens were created around Beijing, where the Emperors and their families could escape the heat of summer. Emperor Qianlong constructed the last of these around Lake Kunming, which had been used as a water supply for more than three thousand years. He extended and deepened the lake, built his Summer Palace beside it and created a garden around it in honour of his mother's birthday. The Summer Palace was destroyed by the Anglo-French Allied Forces during the Second Opium War in 1860 but in the 1880s, Emperor Guangxu reconstructed the garden and Palace on the same site for the use of his mother, the Dowager Empress Cixi. Follow me."

As we approached the first building, three women were just leaving. They were dressed in traditional long flowing robes with long sleeves and each had a huge artificial flower and gold braids in her hair. They looked most attractive. I quickly took a photograph before they vanished into the crowd.

Charles clapped to gain our attention again.

"This is the Hall of Benevolence and Longevity," he informed us. "Inside is the wooden throne on which the Emperor sat to receive visitors and deal with affairs of state. If you look carefully, you will see the carving of a bat which is the symbol of happiness and long life. You have five minutes. Then meet me back here."

We went inside to look around and came back to Charles. When we had all returned, he clapped again and ordered, "Follow me," and we went to the next building.

In the Hall of Happiness in Longevity, we saw the living quarters of the Dowager Empress Cixi, where there was a life-size model of her sitting cross-legged on a bed. Outside were the courtyard and buildings where she kept the young Emperor Guangxu under house arrest, after he led an uprising against her. He died here aged only twenty five.

The Hall of Jade Ripples was where Guangxu had previously stayed with his Empress, while the concubines were housed in the Hall of Yiyun. One of the rooms was full of costumes where visitors could dress up as the Emperor and Empress to be photographed.

My favourite building was the Royal Opera House, situated in one of the courtyards. It had a stage on two levels, connected by four stairways, and the background was painted with clouds and dragons.

The buildings were very attractive on the outside with mainly red facades, rows of red pillars, decorative windows and painted boards under the bamboo roofs, which curved out at the edges and up at the corners, some with rows of good luck figures marching down them.

Inside, however, most of the rooms were nearly bare and looked very poor with plain wooden walls and floors. No doubt at one time there had been silk carpets on the floors and silken brocades, tapestries and paintings lining the wooden walls. It needed a good guide to bring it all to life but Charles, who had seen it all before, stood outside each building and gave us the bare facts before sending us in to have a quick look.

We came to a library which contained a few books. Nearby were the rooms housing the treasures of the Dowager Empress Cixi, which were closed to the public. To see inside, we had to peer through the windows which was easier said than done. The Chinese visitors were all very anxious to view these treasures and not averse to a bit of shoving and pushing, elbowing everybody else out of the way.

We soon discovered that being polite would get us nowhere so David and I followed the example of the locals. Once we had fought our way to a window, we found that reflecting light still made it very difficult to see inside, but from what we were able to glimpse, it was not worth the effort. The treasures looked very meagre.

Charles was really beginning to annoy us, giving us five minutes here and four minutes there, before clapping at us to follow him to the next building. After he had taken us to the main buildings, he told us that we could have forty minutes to wander round by ourselves.

Before we left the hotel that morning, Austin had told us that we would need about three hours to see the grounds of the Summer Palace and for that reason, he usually tried to arrange for an afternoon visit. We rebelled.

"It's not long enough," complained Adrian. "If you allow us an hour, this would bring the meeting time to twelve o'clock."

"I agree," said Gordon.

"Forty minutes won't give us long enough to see anything," said Chris.

Charles looked nonplussed. He was clearly not accustomed to having his authority questioned. However, the rest of us made it clear that we were in general consensus and Charles had no option but to agree. It was a relief to get away from him.

Most of us made our way to Lake Kunming where we found a lovely wooden boat with a large golden dragon's head on the bow and golden bamboo roofs covering the seating area inside.

"I'm going for a walk round the lake," said Adrian. "According to my guide book, there are some interesting bridges at the far end. Would anyone else like to come?"

"I'll join you," said Alan.

"I wouldn't mind having another look round the Palace buildings in my own time," said Julie.

"We'll come with you," said Joanne. "I want to try and get some photos."

The group split up, everyone going their own way.

Across the water, David and I saw two temple buildings rising from the low hillside to our right, but the views were very misty. We decided to walk up to see these temples, from where we hoped we would also see a view of the Summer Palace across the lake. We made our way back past the Hall of Benevolence and Longevity and then through the Harmonious Interest Garden, where there were interestingly shaped limestone rocks, enhanced by ivies with their red autumn colouring.

Behind the palace, steps and footpaths led us up Longevity Hill which was wooded. We kept climbing, hoping to find a clearing near the top, and the path took us above a complex of buildings that made up the Temple of Buddhist Virtue on the far side of the hill. Between the temple buildings, we could see the hazy hills of the countryside in the opposite direction from the lake. A little further along, we found an entrance to the temple complex but knew that we would have insufficient time to see it all.

We continued past it and came to the Cloud Dispelling Hall, an attractive hexagonal multi-storeyed construction overlooking the grey mist of the lake. This was one of the temple buildings we had seen from the lakeside. I took a photograph and from there we walked on along the ridge of the hill towards the Temple of the Sea of Wisdom.

This temple had a green and orange roof, its edges decorated with green good luck figures. Its walls were tiled in an attractive green and orange design, with archways outlined in white marble. Each archway was surrounded by small niches containing Buddha statues but unfortunately, every one had been defaced or decapitated by the Red Guards during the Cultural Revolution. However, the building was still lovely.

"We've got to be back at the lake in twenty minutes," warned David, "and we don't know where the meeting place is yet." Charles had asked us to meet him beside a marble boat that was now used as a restaurant.

"Coming," I said.

As we hurried down the hill by a different path, we were joined by Anna.

"Do you know where the meeting place is?" she asked.

"No," said David. "We need to allow time to find it."

Despite this, when we passed a lower entrance to the Temple of Buddhist Virtue, I could not resist dashing up two flights of steps to photograph the nearest stupa while the other two waited anxiously.

At the bottom of the hill, we went by the entrance to an area that, another visitor told us, had been built as a replica of the Shanghai waterfront. Two sturdy red pillars supporting the magnificent gateway rose from tall white plinths while stone lions reclined round the base of each column. The horizontal boards of the gate were decorated in predominantly blue and gold designs with a rectangular central panel of two golden dragons. We only wished we had more time to explore but I took a quick photograph as we hurried past.

Once we reached the lake, it was not difficult to find the marble boat and we arrived back at the meeting place with Anna and another couple at exactly midday. The rest of the group were waiting but there was no sign of Charles.

It was nearly twenty past twelve when he deigned to put in an appearance. We all clapped at him in annoyance and he looked surprised.

"I thought we had arranged to meet at twelve o'clock," said Phil, annoyed.

"That was your time for meeting up, not mine," he said sarcastically.

He then added, "Because you wanted longer here, there will be no time for you to shop in the market outside. We will have to go straight to the coach to get to the restaurant in time."

If he thought that this would upset us, he was disappointed. None of us had any desire to shop in the market. Charles looked disbelieving when we all walked straight through between the stalls without even slowing to look at anything.

It was nearly an hour's drive from the Summer Palace to the restaurant where we were having lunch. Austin later told us that Charles took every group there. Either it belonged to a friend or relative or he was paid a good commission as there were many excellent restaurants much closer to the Summer Palace.

Lunch was a very slow, leisurely affair and when we were all sitting patiently, waiting to go, Charles told us that we had ten more minutes to enjoy a cigarette after the meal. As none of us smoked, we felt that Charles was going out of his way to annoy us.

Once we were eventually back on the coach and driving towards Beijing, Charles resumed his job as our local guide.

"People working in Xian and Beijing can earn four times as much as those in Canton and nearly everybody has a colour television, refrigerator, freezer, microwave oven and air-conditioning," he said proudly. "Food rationing is a thing of the past. Rationing of rice and flour finished in 1990 and everything can be bought on the open market. The Russians still have rationing and they buy huge quantities of goods on the free market in China and sell them on the black market back home."

"Only a few years ago," he continued, "vegetables were hard to obtain in winter and people had to buy them in bulk during the summer to store for the winter months. Now, fresh and frozen vegetables are available all the year round."

As we came back into Beijing, Charles was telling us, "Nepotism is still very important in China and corruption is rife, although the Government is trying to stamp it out." David nudged me and gave me a meaningful look.

"Our afternoon visit will be to Tiantan, the Temple of Heaven," Charles informed us. "It was built during the Ming Dynasty at the beginning of the fifteenth century and covers three times the area of the Forbidden City. It was here that the Emperor came every year to pray for a good harvest and it was originally known as the Temple of Heaven and Earth."

"In those days," he went on, "the Chinese believed that the Earth was square and Heaven was round and the layout of the temple consists of both squares and circles.

There are four entrances facing north, south, east and west and we shall be entering by the South Gate."

We knew that the Temple of Heaven was less than a twenty minute walk from our hotel because we had passed it the previous evening on our way to Tiananmen Square. David and I were determined not to be rushed this time and as we got off the coach, we told Charles we would make our own way back to the hotel if we wanted to stay longer.

The South Gate consisted of a high red brick wall with three arched entrances and a bamboo roof. Doors sealed the side arches but the central arch stood open. Inside this outer wall stood a row of black metal incense burners.

The path from the gate brought us to two further red walls, this time quite low and roofed with blue pottery cylinders, each with a decorative blue dragon curled within its ceramic end piece. Each of these walls had a trio of double doors set in high marble surrounds.

Only the outer doors stood open in the first wall but we had to use the central entrance in the second wall. I assumed we were zigzagging to confuse the evil spirits. This brought us to a circular, three tiered marble construction that reminded me of a wedding cake.

At the top of each flight of steps leading up the centre of the three tiers was a wide paved terrace surrounded by a marble balustrade. This was made up of rectangular panels, the upper half of each being cut away to leave only an urn-shaped piece of stone in the centre and on either side. From a distance, this gave the stone a lacy appearance. The panels were joined together by marble posts, topped with ornamental cylinders carved with a decorative dragon design. Open-mouthed dragon-head drainpipes projected horizontally round the outside of each of the walls at terrace level.

We climbed the steps to the top, where Charles told us, "This building is the Round Altar. Odd numbers were considered heavenly so there are three entrance gates in each of the perimeter walls and the altar is five metres high. As the largest single odd number, nine, was considered to be the most perfect, there are nine rows of paving at each level. On this top level, there is a central ring of nine stones and each circle of stones around it has a further nine stones so that eighty one stones make up the outermost ring of the top tier. This level symbolised Heaven and when the Emperor stood on the centre stone, the sound of his voice was reflected off the marble balustrades and was magnified, so he sounded as though he were a god."

Charles continued, "Every year, on the day of the Winter Solstice, the Emperor came to this altar to make a sacrifice. He would thank the gods for the past year and ask for all to go well in the coming year. He wore special robes for the ceremony and had to abstain from eating meat beforehand. Every detail of the ceremony had to be carried out with the utmost precision because the slightest mistake meant that the whole country would suffer misfortune in the following year."

We left Heaven, passing through the gates of the double perimeter walls on the north side of the Round Altar. We then passed through another archway and came to the first of the temples, a circular building on a single tier marble base with steps leading up from the four compass points.

Before we went in, Charles called us over to the high circular brick wall curving round the wide courtyard.

"This is the Echo Wall," he told us. "It is sixty five metres across but if one of you stands over here and whispers something against the wall, a person listening on the opposite side will be able to hear it clearly."

"I'm going to try it out," Phil said to Jane. "I'll go across and you can whisper something to me when I get there."

He ran over to the other side, waved, and put his ear to the wall while Jane murmured something in a low voice. When he came back, she asked him, "Could you hear what I was saying?"

"No," said Phil. "I could hear a lot of whispering but couldn't tell what was being said." As several people were whispering along the wall at the same time, this was hardly surprising.

Chris chuckled, "This must be the origin of Chinese Whispers."

Charles now led us across to a stone and asked us to listen carefully. He clapped his hands loudly.

"Did you hear the echoes?"

"I think so," said Liz, doubtfully.

"Listen and I'll do it again," he said. "This is one of the Triple Echo Stones and you should hear the sound echoing three times."

He clapped again and most of us heard, or perhaps imagined, the echoes of the clap.

We now went over to the temple. This was a beautiful building, its wooden circular wall painted in red and gold above which, under a blue tiled roof, was a deep frieze painted in blue, green and yellow, divided into sections with black lines.

"This temple is known as the Imperial Vault of Heaven," Charles told us. "It held the tablets of the

Emperor's ancestors, which were used in the Winter Solstice ceremony. The temple is painted the colours of the five elements, red for fire, blue for air, green for water, yellow for earth and black for wood."

The roof was also patterned although the colours were not so clear. However, below the top where the roof curved up and was completed by a large golden knob, I could make out a faint circle of gold rectangles.

Leading up to the temple, each of the four double flights of steps contained a central sloping block of marble carved with a dragon design. The temple was surrounded by a low marble wall of rectangular panels with marble dragon head drainage pipes, in the same design as we had seen at the Round Altar.

In the courtyard, halfway between the main compass points, stood four large red incense burners, each with a metal canopy. We left the courtyard along a path called the Vermilion Steps Bridge.

"This was also known as the Sacred Way," said Charles, "because the Emperors believed that if they followed it, they could enter Heaven. It leads to the Gate of Prayer for Good Harvests."

The wall of the high Gate was painted red and topped by a deep patterned frieze, predominantly blue in colour, under a long curving bamboo roof with good luck figures at each end. On either side of the gate was a brick wall, more than twenty feet high. The two side entrance arches were sealed with a pair of heavy looking doors but as we approached, we could see the next temple framed in the open central archway.

Going through, we entered another courtyard. Around the temple stood a circle of black metal incense burners, each having a double canopy held up by four metal pillars.

The temple itself was similar in design and with the same colourings as the Imperial Vault of Heaven but was larger and grander. It stood on top of four circular marble tiers and had three blue roofs, one above the other, becoming progressively smaller, with a deep frieze painted in the blue, green, yellow and black design between each roof.

“This is the Temple of Heaven, also known as the Hall of Prayer for Good Harvests,” Charles informed us. “It is thirty eight metres high and thirty metres across, yet there is not a single nail or screw anywhere in its construction. The Temple is made entirely of wood, held together with tongue and groove joints. Among the Emperor’s most important duties was to decide when the fields should be ploughed and the seed planted in the fields and this was where he came to pray for a good harvest. Over to the right, just beyond the Temple, is the abattoir where animals were killed for sacrifice.”

“When you go inside,” he went on, “you will see four columns in the centre representing the four seasons. An inner circle of twelve columns represents the twelve months of the year and an outer circle of twelve columns represents the twelve two-hour periods that make up a day. In the centre of the ceiling is a carved dragon, the symbol of royalty.”

Charles then remained outside while we all went into the temple. The Hall of Prayer for Good Harvests alone would have made our visit worthwhile. It was magnificent. The columns were painted red and gold while wooden boards between the columns, patterned in a broad palette of colours, formed concentric circles up into the roof where the golden dragon curled high in the central dome of the ceiling. Adding to the atmosphere, plaster calves had been placed in wooden troughs to represent the sacrifice for a good harvest.

We were allowed plenty of time to take in all the glory of this building. Before we rejoined Charles, I said to David, "Do you want to stop and see anything again?"

"No," he said. "I didn't feel rushed this afternoon and I'm quite happy to go now."

"Do you realise," I said, "Charles hasn't clapped at us once since we arrived here? Perhaps when we clapped him this morning, he realised how annoying it was."

Back at the hotel, we had time to shower and change before leaving for dinner at five o'clock. After the meal, we were taken to an excellent acrobatic show. In between the acrobatic performances, we were entertained by jugglers and magicians.

The first part of the show seemed a little tame with people balancing on each other's shoulders and turning cartwheels or riding round on unicycles with a variety of articles balanced on their heads. We had been spoilt by seeing similar acts before. However, as the evening went on, the acts became steadily more daring and difficult.

As an example, one man bent over backwards in a crab position supported on his hands and feet, with a nine-rung ladder balanced on his knees, held in place only by a cord held between his teeth.

Another man climbed this ladder while balancing a tall standard lamp on his chin and he then hooked his feet under the rungs of the ladder and leant out horizontally with his arms outstretched, still somehow keeping the standard lamp in position, before making his way back down the ladder. It was the man at the bottom taking all the strain that I really admired.

Thc finalc consisted of eight young men, dressed in green, who performed the most amazing antics around two very high upright poles.

"I daren't watch," whispered Mandy as three of the young men, each supported only by one foot braced against a pole and the other hooked over one of the guy ropes, hung upside down, each spinning a colleague round at arms length, fifteen feet above the stage, or holding him by a cord held between the teeth while he performed various exercises. When we left, we were all on a high, buzzing with excitement.

Back at the hotel, David and I, John, Julie and Chris had entered one of the lifts, designed to hold six people, when Mattie and Josh leapt in, just as the doors were closing. Mattie, the youngest in the group, was talking about the evening and jumping up and down with excitement when the lift, which had started going up, suddenly juddered to a halt.

We pushed the buttons but it refused to go either up or down. John rang the emergency bell and pressed a telephone button over a speaker. A woman answered in Chinese.

"We are with Explore and we are stuck in a lift and need assistance," John said slowly and clearly, while Mattie giggled nervously beside him.

"Shush," David said to her. "They'll think we're playing games."

All went quiet and we waited for five minutes but nothing happened.

"I'll try again," said David and when the woman answered the telephone, after shooting a warning glance at Mattie, he repeated the request.

Again there was the same apparent lack of response and the lift was beginning to get very hot and airless. Mattie started getting hysterical and David told her angrily, "Shut up," which she did.

Chris put his finger on the bell and let it ring continuously until, eventually, a man forced the doors open with a crowbar and we found that we were stuck between floors. "Wait," he said and the doors closed again.

Nothing happened for a while and Mattie looked as though she was going to start screaming and crying again until one glare from David stopped her. Then the lift began to descend and continued until the indicator showed -2. The lift then moved slowly back up from the sub-basement to the ground floor, the doors opened and we were free.

As we staggered out in relief, John said, "I'm not going to risk going up in another lift. I'm taking the stairs."

"There's only one lift working anyway," I said, noticing that one of the others now had an 'Out of Order' sign on it. Although our rooms were up on the eighth floor, we had had enough excitement for one evening and took our time going up the stairs.

Summer Palace

Tiantan, Temple of Heaven

Entrance to Ming tombs

Selling persimmons

Wednesday 27th October

When we were ready to go down for breakfast, there was still only one lift working, so we used the stairs after making sure that we had with us everything we were likely to need for the day. After the meal, Charles met us in the lobby and we set off early with great anticipation to visit one of the Ming tombs and the Great Wall.

On the journey, Charles told us, "Thirteen of the sixteen Ming Emperors were buried in an area bounded by a river and two guardian mountains called Tiger and Dragon but Dingling is the only Ming tomb that has been excavated. It is the tomb of Emperor Wan Li who died in 1620 and is the second largest in the valley. It was built during the Emperor's lifetime and when it was completed, he celebrated by holding a party inside."

"That sounds rather macabre," laughed Alan.

The coach parked outside the entrance to the area containing the thirteen Ming tombs, covering many square kilometres. Fortunately, it was not far to Wan Li's tomb. We went through a white gate first and then a red gate.

The red gate consisted of three archways in a high red-painted wall with a bamboo tiled roof. It was similar to the entrance to Tiantan that we had seen the previous day, except that all three entrances were open and there was a backdrop of misty mountains. The central archway framed the curving roofs of Dingling mausoleum, rising above the treetops.

The wide paved pathway leading from the gate to the tomb had orchards of peach and apple trees on either side and the land appeared to be very fertile. The entrance to the tomb was through a square red building with a double roof, each roof layer having its own good luck symbols.

"This building is known as the Soul Tower," Charles informed us.

To enter the tomb, we went down one hundred and fifty stone steps and at the bottom, came to a bare tunnel.

"This reminds me of the London Underground," I said to Jess who was standing next to me.

"Doesn't it just," she agreed. "I can almost feel the warm rush of air as a tube train approaches the station."

We turned off into a passage with a hole in the floor called the 'Golden Well' into which Chinese visitors threw their money. This passage led to the main hall of the tomb in which stood three white marble thrones, each provided with a yellow porcelain candle holder and a blue and white porcelain vase. To the right of these were three red wooden cube-shaped boxes, about three feet high, that may have been coffins but looked as though they should each contain a Jack-in-the-Box. To the left were three replica skeletons in glass cases … and that was it! I was not impressed.

"When the tomb was first opened," Charles clarified, "the coffins were surrounded by chunks of uncut jade, thought to have the power to preserve the dead, plus several trunks of objects, including cookery books. Copies of some of these objects were kept in the tomb when the originals were moved to museums for safekeeping, but were destroyed by the Red Guards during the Cultural Revolution."

We left the underground tunnel by a different route and climbed about two hundred steps, coming out into a square arched building with a terrace and views down over the parapet to the long entrance walk below. From here we followed a curving pathway, with very pleasant views of the mountainous scenery behind the tomb.

As we made our way back to the coach, we had time to watch a young couple playing Chinese badminton, where the shuttlecock stuck to the racquet with a suction pad if caught correctly. We then walked through a collection of stalls.

There were lovely, if rather flimsy, paper kites for sale in the shape of butterflies. A small boy was gazing in fascination at a battery-operated toy racing cyclist pedalling madly round in circles. Further on, a stallholder was selling clockwork birds. He wound them up with a key and then released them to fly up into the trees and circle a couple of times before dive-bombing the spectators below as the spring unwound.

A group of minority people dressed in red held an ornate sedan chair. From its four blue carrying bars hung lengths of red satin with gold fringing and the box-like sedan chair was painted red and gold. Its pitched roof, which was covered in red and gold satin with gold tassels, had doll figures standing all round the edge and a fancy golden crown in the centre.

A percussion band beat out a rhythm and passers-by were being cajoled to pay for a ride in the chair. We saw a man climb in but instead of walking down the path with him, the bearers stood on the spot and bounced him up and down in the chair for a few minutes to the rhythm of the band.

We found all these amusements far more interesting than the tomb. As we left, we passed a brass plaque in a marble surround informing us that we had visited one of the 'Forty Topping Tourist Attractions of China'.

Outside the tomb area, on our way back to the coach, we saw some persimmons for sale, piled up on top of the wall. These fruits were a speciality of the region and were included in our lunch that day at a nearby restaurant. I was still rather put off by their appearance, like very squashy, rotten tomatoes, but having already tasted one a few days earlier in Xian, I knew that the flesh inside was delicious.

When we arrived at the restaurant, we found that it was very attractive, light and airy with open courtyards.

"This looks a nice place," approved Alan. Then we saw a movement to one side.

"Uh oh, there's a rat!" exclaimed Liz.

"There's another one over there," Julie pointed out.

We were shown to tables outside and when we sat, we tucked our legs under us on the chairs to avoid being bitten but, otherwise, we tried to ignore the rodents.

After the meal, the coach took us to the Great Wall. On the way there, Charles was explaining to us that there was no concept of privacy in China.

"People will not hesitate to ask the most personal questions," he told us. "Businessmen travelling abroad or receiving foreign visitors have to be taught that Westerners value their own space and that they should not look through their bags, briefcases or desk drawers without permission."

Further on, he began telling us about Neighbourhood Committees.

"These are a feature of Chinese society," he said. "They are made up of retired people selected by the local Council, who may choose to pick those they know to be good Communists. It is the responsibility of these Committee members to look after the elderly and handicapped, organise crèches and kindergartens, and deal with marital disputes and quarrels between neighbours. They are even responsible for sorting out problems such as pest control. However, while there's a great deal of social benefit, these Committees also act as spies. They can easily identify anyone who doesn't toe the line and, as one of their tasks is to welcome newcomers to the area, it's impossible for a stranger to go unnoticed."

He then gave us some information about the legal system.

"The old legal system was completely destroyed during the Cultural Revolution and new laws are being brought in all the time," he said. "There are three levels of court so although, for example, a suspected murderer would first be tried at middle court level, there is a higher court to which he can appeal."

While Charles was talking, I was looking out of the window at the scenery. Along the roadside, the autumn colours of stag's horn sumach, which was growing wild, made lovely vivid splashes of scarlet against the grey-green landscape. Our coach passed a train which was ambling along at about twenty miles an hour and Charles told us that it was the Trans-Mongolian Express. We then saw a large stone wall trailing over the mountains.

"Look," said Adrian, "there's the Great Wall."

"No," Charles corrected him. "That is one of the inner walls, used to separate the different states of China prior to unification. During the Qin Dynasty in about 200 BC, these walls were linked and strengthened. Legend has it that one of the building materials used was the bodies of deceased workers."

"The Great Wall itself stretches for about five thousand kilometres and is one of the features of Earth that can be seen from space," Charles went on. "It was first built from compacted earth nearly two thousand years ago but between the fourteenth and seventeenth centuries, during the Ming Dynasty, the Great Wall was reconstructed using brick and stone. It later fell into disrepair and people took away many of the bricks and stones for other building work but parts of the Great Wall have been restored recently as one of China's major tourist attractions. We are about to visit a stretch of the Great Wall at Badaling, which is one of the main tourist sites."

We arrived shortly afterwards. From the coach park, a ten minute walk took us up the road and under a bridge, guarded by two men in very colourful mediaeval uniforms with wide-brimmed tin helmets.

In front of the entrance to the Wall, the Wu Diao Circus had set up camp. They had carpeted the ground in front of their tent, a live orchestra was playing and a very energetic dancing display was in full swing. However, there was no time to linger as we were on a group ticket to the Great Wall and Charles was hurrying us along.

When we joined the queue at the entrance, Charles told us that we had three hours to explore and make our own way back to the coach.

“I’ve been told that the best views are to the left, once we get on to the Wall,” said Austin, who was coming with us. Accordingly, once inside, we all turned to the left.

Most visitors were turning to the right from the entrance which took them to a nearby watchtower, with views of the Wall snaking up and over the nearest hills. Four models of guardsmen stood there in copper-coloured armour.

“That way looks interesting,” said David. I agreed.

“We’ll leave enough time to go up to the watchtower when we come back.”

To the left of the entrance was a brick barrier across the Wall, with a low arch flanked by another two guards in mediaeval dress, waiting to have their photographs taken with the visitors. I thought they would check our tickets but they just grinned at us as we ducked through the arch.

As might be expected, the part of the Wall nearest to the Badaling entrance was very touristy. Minority tribe guards in colourful outfits holding pikes and halberds were on duty at every watchtower, encouraging tourists to be photographed with them, while others from the minority tribes were pushing us to buy postcards which, like everywhere else in China, were only available in packs of ten. There were T-shirts for sale proclaiming ‘I climbed the Great Wall’ and I saw some heavy-looking metal coins, circular with a square hole cut out of the centre.

We were welcomed to one tower with loud drumming. The single guard had a large, rather worn, red-sided drum held upright in a frame and he seemed to be enjoying himself beating out a tattoo on his instrument.

Although the clouds were low and the hills were misty, it was dry and we could see the Wall stretching away into the distance. As it undulated up and down the hills, it snaked from side to side and for about a mile, it was decorated with flags on poles attached to the parapet on either side.

There was a drop of about twenty five feet to the base of the Wall, with the hillside falling away below that, so it must have provided quite a formidable defence system. The top was paved and Austin told us that the width was sufficient to allow five men on horseback to ride side by side.

Usually when walls are built up a slope, the rows of bricks remain horizontal but on parts of the Great Wall, the bricks were laid parallel to the ground which gave the Wall a fluid appearance as it followed the lie of the land.

Some sections were very steep and tiring to climb. Handrails had been fastened to the parapet walls and in the steepest parts, the slope changed to steps which were very narrow in depth and up to two feet high. Parents were having to carry their children up the steps because they could not cope with the height.

We were wearing walking boots and when we were coming down the steep sections, we were grateful for the handrail because, unless we placed our feet sideways, only the heels of our boots would fit on the steps and it would have been easy to fall, particularly as the weather was now closing in and the paving stones were getting very damp and slippery.

When we reached the tower that marked the highest point on this section of the Wall, signed certificates were on sale to affirm that the holder had climbed the Great Wall. The flags ended here becausc fcw visitors wanted to walk beyond this point. When we looked back, we were amazed to see how high we had climbed from the entrance gate in the valley far below. However, it was now drizzling quite hard so the view was very hazy.

There were one or two visitors on the next short stretch of the Wall but after that, it was deserted apart from our group. We continued on to the very end of the reconstructed part of the Wall.

"We are now going to walk on part of the original Wall," said Austin. "Please be careful, because much of it has crumbled away and the ground is very uneven."

We had to scramble down to the old Wall, which was at a lower level than the reconstruction. We all followed Austin but it was quite difficult to walk along the top. After a short distance, what remained of the Wall deteriorated even further and our friends had to clamber down on to a path that ran alongside.

"Do you want to go any further?" I asked David. It was now raining quite hard and the views were shrouded in mist.

"No," he said. "I'm glad we can say we've walked on the original Wall but I think I've seen enough. The path isn't even on the Wall now. Let's go back."

Austin had already told us all that we could turn back at any time so there was no need to inform him first. As expected, we arrived back at the entry point with plenty of spare time.

“Do you really want to go up the other side?” asked David. “There’s a café near the entrance where we could shelter and dry out.”

“We’ll probably never come to the Great Wall again,” I said, “so I’d like to go at least as far as the first watchtower while we’re here.”

“OK,” David agreed reluctantly.

However, once we had started to climb the Wall in the other direction, we continued as far as the fourth watchtower, which was the highest point on that side. We decided that Austin had been right and that we had seen the best views by going left.

Back at the entrance, we still had a short time to spare so we made our way to the café, where we sat in the dry until the rest of the group came down. They were bubbling with excitement.

“It was wonderful walking along the old Wall,” Jess enthused. “There was so much atmosphere. You could just imagine being a defender, facing warring hordes coming over the mountains.”

We returned to the coach and on the way back to Beijing, as it was now late afternoon, we stopped at a restaurant on the outskirts of the city for our evening meal.

“Just wait here while I go and check where we’re sitting,” said Charles. We stood outside the entrance for fifteen minutes while other tour groups arrived and were allowed inside.

“I’ll find out what’s happening,” said Austin at last. He entered the restaurant and a few more minutes passed but he eventually reappeared, followed by Charles.

"What's the problem?" asked Gordon, getting annoyed.

"Apparently Charles booked our tables for the wrong time, so we can't get in," Austin told us, calmly. "He now has to ring round to try and find a restaurant with enough space to accommodate us all. We might as well sit in the coach while we're waiting."

It was another ten minutes before Charles was successful and we set off in the coach again. We arrived at the restaurant and were shown to our seats but we soon discovered that, because we had not been expected, the restaurant was short of food. They brought us what they had but we cleared all the plates and were still hungry when we left. Austin negotiated a reduction in the meal price for us but this incident had done nothing to enhance Charles' standing.

On the way back to the hotel, Austin announced, "You'll be delighted to hear that I've managed to obtain a screwdriver. If you all stay in your rooms this evening, I'll come round to each of you in turn to take the locks off one of the windows and let some fresh air in." We cheered and clapped. The heat at night had been almost unbearable.

Austin reached our room by about eight o'clock. As soon as he had the locks off, we opened the window wide and the stream of cool air felt wonderful. It was such a relief.

Once Austin had gone, Li Mei came to our room to teach us how to play Mah-Jong, using the set we had purchased in Chengdu, so we had an interesting evening.

Thursday 28th October

After breakfast, we went to visit the Forbidden City. This time, the coach took us most of the way there but from where it was parked, we had a ten minute walk in a torrential downpour. The roads were flooded and passing vehicles sprayed us with water.

We escaped from the roads as we crossed Tiananmen Square but there was no shelter and, in any case, by now we were thoroughly drenched. At the end of the Square, we went down a subway which took us under the road and by the time we had come up the steps outside the Forbidden City, miraculously the rain had stopped and the sun was shining.

Charles took us to the central archway in the high red wall with the picture of Mao over the entrance, purchased our tickets and handed us one each before leaving. We were now free for the rest of the day.

The ticket was a very smart affair in cardboard, measuring more than seven inches by three inches, on the front of which was a picture of the Summer Palace, the lake filled with rowing boats. There was also a large inset circular metal coin with a square hole cut out of the centre, around which was the engraving of a dragon and a fish.

We walked through Tiananmen or the Gate of Heavenly Peace, which was set within the Meridian Gate building, and into a courtyard that was so wet after the heavy rain that it looked like a lake, particularly with the sunshine reflecting off the surface. In front of us, five marble bridges crossed a small stream.

The Great Wall

Entrance to the Forbidden City

Pavilion, Longtan Park

We went over the central bridge and came to a long building standing on a marble platform and consisting of a row of arches topped by a two tiered roof. This was the Gate of Supreme Harmony and was where each of us was given headphones and a cassette player, with a tape recording by Roger Moore who would guide us through the Forbidden City. The tape could be stopped or replayed as required, so we could each go through in our own time, far better than Charles giving us five minutes here and four minutes there and clapping at us.

Roger Moore began by telling us that the Forbidden City was so called because, although visitors were allowed into the outer area, the penalty was death for anyone who dared to enter the main palace area, other than the Emperor, his family, concubines and authorised palace staff.

Construction of the Forbidden City began during the Ming Dynasty in 1407 AD and was said to have taken a million workers fourteen years to complete. Marble was quarried from just outside Beijing and was slid into the city on ice during the winter but other materials had to be transported further.

The red city wall, more than eight metres thick at the base, was reputed to have been built using a mixture of white lime and sticky rice, cemented together with egg whites, which made it very strong. After completion, the Forbidden City was occupied by twenty four Ming and Qing Emperors until 1911, when the last Qing Emperor, Pu Yi, had to learn to adapt to life outside as an ordinary citizen.

We had entered the complex through the central entrance of the Meridian Gate. This would have been reserved for the Emperor with lesser mortals using the four smaller side entrances. The Emperor would have been carried through the Gate on his sedan chair to the sound of gongs and bells and from here, he would review his armies in the square outside and would also pass judgement on prisoners, watch public floggings and announce the New Year calendar.

The five marble bridges had taken us across the Golden Stream, which was shaped like a Tartar's bow and was spanned by another five marble bridges within the complex. The pillars on the bridges were shaped like torches.

Round the outside of the Forbidden City was the palace moat. Being constructed of wood, the palace regularly went up in flames so the moat came in handy, as the local Fire Brigade was considered far too common to extinguish the Royal fires.

Having heard Roger Moore's introduction, we left the Gate of Supreme Harmony and crossed another courtyard to the Hall of Supreme Harmony. We learnt that this courtyard, flanked by green incense burners, could hold an Imperial audience of up to ten thousand people.

The Hall of Supreme Harmony looked almost identical to its Gate except that it had three tiers of marble staircases, guarded by a large bronze lion and lioness on marble pedestals. The marble terraces were each equipped with the usual dragon-head drainage system, which perhaps partly accounted for why the courtyard was so wet. Up the middle of the central staircase, closed to the public, was a massive marble slab carved with dragons, similar to those we had seen at Tiantan, the Temple of Heaven.

"The Hall of Supreme Harmony was the largest and most important building in the complex," Roger Moore's cultured tones informed us. "It was used for ceremonious occasions such as coronations, the Emperor's birthday, Royal weddings and New Year celebrations." Military and Court processions would also make their way up the steps and on to the marble terraces.

Located to the west of the Hall of Supreme Harmony was a grain measure and to the east a sundial, both representing imperial justice. Outside, its head held high, stood a large bronze turtle, the symbol of longevity. This was actually an incense burner and when it was in use, fragrant smoke would billow from its mouth.

We were prevented from entering the Hall but peering across the barriers, we could make out the Dragon Throne where the Emperor held audience. All his decisions were final, with no right of appeal. The pillars in front of the throne were decorated with gold lacquer and dragons, the symbol of imperial majesty.

When the Emperor entered and sat on his throne, to the banging of drums and gongs, everyone present had to hit the floor nine times with his forehead. Having done this, surrounded by all the noise and the smoke from the incense burners drifting through the Hall, the visitors and courtiers must have felt quite disorientated. We walked round the Hall of Supreme Harmony and found some very large and beautiful bronze bowls.

In front of us across the next courtyard, the smaller Hall of Middle Harmony stood on a single marble terrace and looked more like a gateway, with an opening on either side through to the next courtyard. Two broad stairways led to the openings. The middle flight of steps, leading to the closed area of the Hall, had a long central slab of marble, carved with a dragon design and guarded by a shining golden lion on both sides. The large golden bowls at either end of the building were probably used as incense burners.

In the Hall of Middle Harmony, Roger informed us, the Emperor would have prepared for ceremonies in the Hall of Supreme Harmony, rehearsing his speeches and holding discussions with high ranking Government officials. The Emperor also inspected the ploughs in this Hall and he himself would plough the first furrow in a selected field.

Inside the Hall of Middle Harmony stood two sedan chairs from the Qing Dynasty in which the Emperors would have been carried around the Forbidden City. However, the last Qing Emperor, Pu Yi, preferred the bicycle as a far faster and more convenient means of transport.

Behind the Hall of Middle Harmony stood the Hall of Preserving Harmony, this time on a three-tiered marble base and with the usual marble slab carved with dragons in the central flight of steps. This was where scholars sat the extremely competitive civil service examinations. They were tested by the Emperor himself and those that passed were guaranteed a Government position.

All three of these Halls would have been used for banquets while the smaller buildings to the sides of the main halls would have been used for storing gold and silver, silks and brocades, carpets and other finery needed for various ceremonies.

The palace was divided into two areas, the outer public area, the Yan, representing the male and Heaven, the circular shape of the coin on our entrance ticket, and the private inner area, the Yin, representing the female and the Earth, the square hole cut from the centre of the coin. The south, in the direction of the entrance, was also associated with the male and with fire, the north with the female and water.

The next building, the Gate of Heavenly Purity, marked the end of the public part of the Forbidden City. Only the Emperor, his wives and concubines were allowed beyond this point. Not even the royal princes could enter.

Every morning at six o'clock, the Emperor would come to the Gate of Heavenly Purity to receive the reports of his Ministers and make decisions. This was to prove that the Emperor worked hard. It also tested the loyalty of his Ministers who often had to leave home by three o'clock every morning to be there on time. A marble walkway led to the central opening of this Gate and incense burners stood along the single marble platform in front of the Gate.

Beyond the Gate were three more main buildings, the Palace of Heavenly Purity, the Hall of Union and Peace and the Palace of Earthly Tranquillity. The Hall of Union and Peace was where the Empress held her birthday celebrations and, as guardian of the art of spinning and weaving, fed the first mulberry leaves of the year to the silkworms.

The good luck figures along the edges of the roofs of these buildings included a figure mounted on a hen with his retreat cut off by a procession of real and mythical animals. These related to a tyrannical prince of the Han

Dynasty who was hung from a roof. As well as being symbols of good luck and protection, they served as a constant reminder to the Emperor of the dangers of misusing his imperial power.

Around the courtyard surrounding these three buildings were the quarters of the concubines, chosen girls aged between twelve and fifteen. The Emperor had twenty seven bedrooms set up and would move from one to another.

A eunuch would bring a plate of tablets, each bearing the number of a wife or concubine and the Emperor selected from these at random. The eunuch on duty would then find the 'lucky' lady who was stripped naked, to ensure that she was not carrying a weapon, before she was wrapped in a yellow cloth, carried to the designated Royal boudoir and dumped unceremoniously at the feet of the Emperor. The eunuch would then record the time and date. Should any of his wives or concubines become pregnant, this record enabled the Emperor to check on the legitimacy of the child.

To be a eunuch was seen as a way of advancement for the sons of poor families. The 'Royal chop' was administered with a sharp knife at a eunuch clinic near the Forbidden City but about half those operated on died shortly afterwards. As mutilation was considered to be grounds for exclusion from the after-life, many eunuchs carried their appendage in a pouch in the hope that, when they eventually died, this would deceive the heavenly spirits.

The Palace of Earthly Tranquillity was a plain building used for religious ceremonies and sacrificial offerings. Lambs, pigs and oxen were slaughtered, cooked, offered and then eaten.

Close by was the Imperial Wedding Chamber where the Emperor and Empress spent the first three nights after their marriage. The walls were painted red for good fortune, while the decorative boardings under the eaves were painted in patterns of blue, green, yellow and black, the other elemental colours. Inside, red lanterns hung from the ceiling.

Beyond the courtyard surrounding these buildings were the Imperial Gardens. As nobody other than the Emperor and Empress could leave the confines of the Forbidden City, these gardens must have been essential to the mental well-being of the occupants.

When the Emperor did venture forth, it was only after taking every precaution. The Court was placed under military guard and secret servicemen lined the route and all roads leading to it. When travelling, the Emperor was not only completely hidden from view but chose at random one of many palanquins in the procession, so that the public had no way of knowing which one he occupied.

The gardens contained the usual flower arrangements made up of dozens of pot plants and shrubs in containers. The sunshine was now long gone and a cold wind was blowing as we hurried round, trying to see everything. There were pools surrounded by low marble walls, beautified with weirdly shaped pieces of worn limestone and patches of water lilies. Buildings were ornamented with red pillars and many had bamboo roofs painted blue and gold with golden good luck figures.

Within the gardens, behind railings, stood a very large incense burner. This must have had a reputation for bringing good luck, because the Chinese were all trying to throw their money inside the burner and the ground around it was littered with coins and small denomination notes. A wishing well in China would soon make its owner a small fortune.

There was also a symbolic limestone mountain with a pavilion on top. It is a tradition in China that, on the ninth of September, everybody climbs a hill to see the countryside and the autumn colourings. Thus, every year on the ninth of September, the Emperor and Empress would climb up to the pavilion from where they were able to see across the city to the Western Hills.

“Look, there’s a café,” said David. “I’m cold. I could do with a hot drink.”

We were still damp from the early morning drenching and with the chilly wind, we felt frozen. The doors of the café were open so we went inside and sat down. We were the only customers but although the staff were serving each other with tea and coffee, they deliberately ignored us.

“It must be their lunch break,” I decided.

“Do you want to see any more of the gardens or shall we leave?” asked David.

“I think we’ve seen everything already,” I said. “Let’s go and have a hot meal somewhere.”

We handed back our cassette tapes and headphones at the exit Gate of Divine Military Genius and headed east to Wangfujing, which Austin had told us was Beijing’s equivalent of London’s Oxford Street.

“I can see a sign for the Holiday Inn,” I said. “Let’s go in there and look at their menu.”

The hotel was warm and relaxing inside and we treated ourselves to a comforting hot thick broth containing meat and vegetables, served with a warm roll and butter, followed by coffee and chocolate truffles. After the meal, David sighed contentedly. "I feel much better now," he said.

We had warmed up and dried out over the meal. We made use of the toilet facilities and found hot water and warm towels – what luxury! We then each decided to have a slice of chocolate cream cake and another coffee, which this time was served with macaroons. The bill came to the equivalent of £15.00 but it was worth every penny. Feeling fully recovered, we went to explore the Beijing shops.

At that time, we collected stamps as souvenirs from each country we visited, so we went to find the Post Office first. Here, we had great fun trying to buy two of each stamp that they had in stock. Once the woman at the first counter understood what it was we wanted, she explained to her colleagues and we then went to each of the three counters in turn to show the stamps we had already collected, so that they could check whether they had any that were different. At the third counter, we paid for them all and the cashier put the stamps into an envelope to protect them.

Our next task was to search out a candy shop, as we both worked in offices where it was the custom to take back sweets for colleagues from whichever country was visited. We found a lovely food shop where the stock included candies, nuts and glacé fruits of all kinds. Even better, we were allowed to sample some of these before making our purchases.

Having completed our shopping, we now explored the stores in general. We enjoyed going round a toyshop where David tried out a gun that shot bubbles and I played with a panda that walked or stopped at the sound of a handclap. I had been told that cashmere sweaters were very cheap in China but when we found a shop that sold them, we calculated that they cost £120.00 each, which was not what we considered a bargain.

By now, the weather had brightened up again, so we made our way back to Tiananmen Square to take photographs of the outside of the Forbidden City and of the Square.

“Do you want to go round the Mao Mausoleum?” asked David.

“Not really,” I said. “It’s getting late anyway. I think I’d rather go back and have time to relax, have a shower and change for the evening.” We crossed the Square and took a taxi back to the hotel.

When we first arrived in Beijing, Austin had asked us all whether we would like to experience a Chinese opera and we had all been very enthusiastic. The previous evening, when he had come round to each of our rooms, he told us, “I had a word with Charles about booking seats for the opera but he wanted to charge such a high rate of commission that I refused. Although it is frowned on, I made the booking myself and we have seats for tomorrow night. We’ll be collected from Reception after we return from the evening meal. Please don’t breathe a word to Charles.”

That evening, we were taken for miles by coach to the outskirts of the city, to eat in one of Charles’s chosen restaurants. After the meal, we were brought back to the hotel and Charles left.

“I’ve hired a yellow minivan to take us to the opera to keep the costs down,” Austin told us. “It’s the cheapest form of transport in Beijing." The minivan arrived to pick us up about fifteen minutes later.

Austin had managed to get seats for us in the front row of the balcony. We had not known quite what to expect but soon discovered that Chinese opera was very different from anything we had seen or heard before.

The first part of the opera was a long drawn-out saga with an inconclusive ending and involved a young man, a girl, a matchmaker and a jade bracelet. It was chanted in very high pitched wailing tones with drums and cymbals clashing in the background. The costumes were beautiful and the make-up lavish, with red eye shadow on white faces.

This was followed by a very lively story of good versus evil, incorporating some extremely clever stylised fighting. As one man battled against seven or eight adversaries, they threw weapons to each other in a masterpiece of choreography and timing, with a mixture of juggling, dancing and acrobatics. After this truly excellent performance, which regrettably only lasted just over an hour, we made our way back to the hotel.

As this was our last night in Beijing, we had all arranged to meet in the bar of the hotel at half past nine for a final get-together. Alan had been nominated to make a speech, thanking Austin for being an excellent leader and for helping to make our holiday so memorable. At the end of the speech, Austin was presented with a Great Wall coin, a Great Wall T-shirt with a cap to match in red and white, plus a 'Passport to Beijing' card which we had all signed.

It was then Alan's turn to be surprised as his birthday was the following day. About an hour early, we all sang him 'Happy Birthday' and Mandy presented him with a toy panda which he promptly christened Bo-Bo, plus a Great Wall T-shirt which we had all signed using a felt-tipped pen, including Li Mei who had signed in Chinese script.

Much to the amazement of a group of Germans from Heidelberg who were also staying at our hotel, both men then stripped to the waist to try on their T-shirts and did a little dance of celebration. It was a good finish to the final evening of our holiday.

Friday 29th October

The next morning, David and I found that both our bath and toilet had become blocked overnight so while we were having breakfast and packing, we had the plumbers in. We then had an hour and a half to spare before leaving for the airport at eleven o'clock, so we decided to have a look around Longtan Park which was not far away.

It was a beautiful, clear sunny morning but bitterly cold, particularly after the stifling heat of the Tiantan Hotel, and we could see our breath in the frosty air as we walked down the road to the park. On the left side of the road was a funfair which looked closed. On the right stood a magnificent entrance gate to the park, with two large golden dragons hanging from the eaves below the bamboo roof. We paid our entrance fee which was minimal and made our way towards a lake at the centre.

This was a lovely place. At one end, there were limestone rocks up to twenty feet high, but differing in size and split into crags and pinnacles. Some of the smaller rocks in front formed islands in the lake.

Between the rocks, a few of which were decorated with tendrils of red ivy, grew various shrubs and trees including a beautiful weeping willow. Everything was reflected in the still, clear water, creating an atmosphere of great tranquillity.

Following a path round the lake, we came to bridges, pagodas and stepping stones across the water. In a clearing, we found a ram with a red ribbon tied in a bow on top of its head and a red cloth over its back, harnessed to a small two-wheeled carriage. It stood patiently waiting to take children for a ride, while its owner sat on a nearby stone seat at a stone table, reading the morning newspaper.

There were side paths through the shrubbery, some of which led to interesting discoveries. Down one of these we found a Dragon Clock. This stood on a marble pillar, about eight feet high, carved with intricate twisting dragons. A single dragon, similar in shape to a Welsh dragon, stood on top of the clock, which was stopped at half past six.

Down another path, a dragon's head with long fangs threatened us from the shrubbery. A third path led to a long pavilion with an undulating roof in gold bamboo with green edgings and ridge tiles on which stood golden dragons. This roof was supported by sturdy red pillars around which were wrapped honey-coloured dragons. The open building stood on a marble base and inside, a lone young woman was practising tai chi.

We passed several men carrying birdcages with their birds inside, some with covers over them, some open to the air, the Chinese equivalent of taking the dog for a walk.

At one place, the lake narrowed and there was a small garden of low flowering shrubs beyond which was the water, with a collection of rocks on the opposite shore looking like a miniature city of rocky skyscrapers.

We then came to an area where the lake narrowed while the path beside it widened into a paved area. In front of us stood a white limestone bridge with marble balustrades. It crossed the lake in a single high semicircular stone arch and an art class of four young students had brought their own folding wooden stools with them and were sitting on these, trying to paint a picture of the bridge. The teacher's example was on display for the novices to look at if they needed guidance.

Further round the lake, we came to a much longer bridge, in the centre of which stood a double pagoda. Beyond this, in the distance, we could see the skyscrapers of Beijing, many probably containing Company flats for long-serving employees. Li Mei had told us that the Government rented flats out to its own workforce for the equivalent of about £2.00 a month.

Although we were tempted to keep walking, time was now running short so we made our way back to the hotel. Here we found that Jane and Phil had been with Julie and Chris to visit Mao's tomb in Tiananmen Square.

"After queuing with the Chinese for nearly an hour," Julie told me, "we entered the Mausoleum where armed guards kept everyone moving, so we were through and out again in about a minute."

"Mao's preserved body was displayed in a crystal coffin in a roped-off area at a darkened end of the mausoleum," Jane put in. "We only glimpsed it for a second or two and I reckon it was a waxwork model."

"The Chinese didn't look either excited or sad to see Mao," added Phil. "They were totally expressionless as they filed past."

David and I had become good friends with Li Mei, our National Guide, so David had been chosen to make the vote of thanks and present her with the usual sealed envelope filled with tips. She then left to travel to Xian to see her husband for a few days before joining another group as National Guide. It was also time to say goodbye to John, our Canadian friend, who was travelling on to Shanghai, Wuxi and Hangzhou.

At eleven o'clock, the rest of us set off in the coach and stopped on the way to the airport for an early lunch at the New Ark restaurant. As Alan, who was celebrating his birthday, actually came from Newark, this seemed a very appropriate place for our last meal in China. Harry and Lucille were not leaving until the following day and said their farewells after the meal, having arranged transport back into the centre of Beijing.

We arrived at the airport at half past twelve. Phil had been designated as the person to give Charles his tips envelope but as there was rather less than usual in it, he wisely waited until we had all unloaded our luggage and were ready to go inside. Austin showed us where to check in but then had to rush off to catch an Aeroflot flight via Moscow. We had presented him with his tips envelope the previous evening.

Those of us returning to Heathrow were unable to check our luggage in until a quarter to three so we took it in turns to guard the cases while the others walked round the airport. We were not allowed to take our FECs out of the country so one of our tasks was to visit the airport Bank. Unfortunately, they had run out of sterling so we had to change our FECs to dollars at a very poor rate of exchange.

We flew home with Pakistan Airlines, leaving Beijing at twenty to five that evening and reaching Islamabad at eleven o'clock at night. Here we had six hours to wait but an airport restaurant was opened up for the sole use of our group.

We were given food and drink and after the meal, we chatted for a while. Jenny then pulled a pack of cards out of her backpack. A few games of rummy were followed by stretching exercises which passed the time quite well. Anita and Anna showed off their skills at yoga, both being extremely flexible.

We had a further stop in Dubai where we were allowed off the aircraft for half an hour to stretch our legs. We finally arrived at Heathrow on Saturday morning, at nine twenty British Summer Time, twenty past four in the afternoon Beijing time. Once we had collected our luggage, we said our farewells and went our separate ways.

. . . . . .

The following Christmas, we all exchanged cards and David and I had two lovely surprises.

Mandy had created a wonderful montage of all the members of the group, made up of cuttings from various photographs, and she had sent one to each of us with a Christmas card.

We were then amazed and delighted to receive a Chinese Christmas card from Li Mei. As she must have been either a local or national guide for many tour groups during the course of the year, we felt highly honoured to be remembered in this way. Both items were added to our souvenirs of a wonderful holiday.

By the same Author

From Coconuts to Condors

"'They're going to throw those!' David said urgently. Carol was just assuring him that he was worrying unnecessarily when the first stones came hurtling across at the party. Our Official City Guide immediately retaliated by picking up cobble stones himself and hurling them back at the youths..."

This was just one of many unexpected incidents, such as having to sleep in a blood-spattered hotel room or being served a meal of inedible llama meat followed by fizzy fruit salad, that made this trip to Brazil, Peru and Bolivia so unforgettable.

A nice travelogue, honest and lightly written. It's warts and all. "The entrance and archway dating back to the 16th century had obviously been used more recently as a public convenience. It smelt dreadful..." If you want an insight into travel through Brazil, Peru and Bolivia, this will give you what you're after.

Paul Bondsfield, Explore Worldwide

As a fellow traveller to the Andes, I have much enjoyed 'From Coconuts to Condors'. I don't actually mind the photos being in black and white, as I can visualise the locations from Valerie's excellent descriptive writing. I have also enjoyed the fact that the book is well written, in the correct tense, and with proper punctuation! Having only been to Peru, I now want to visit both Brazil and Bolivia! Thank you Valerie.

Gill Twissell, author of 'Rest Upon the Wind'

.....one of the best travel books I have read – full of detail, never boring and more like a wonderful adventure story. I really admire not only your bravery in going to such dangerous places, but also your stamina in coping with food poisoning and making such early morning departures. Thank you again for such a delightful read..

Lynda Mitchell, Lincoln Book Festival

…..a marvellous account of a challenging three week holiday in Brazil, Peru and Bolivia. Her very readable writing style makes the culture, climate and landscapes of these countries come to life. Her descriptions are incredibly detailed and picturesque, making it so easy to visualise the scenes that she describes. Indeed, I almost felt as though I was in the shower with her and the little green frogs! …..I thoroughly enjoyed this delightful travelogue - well worth reading, even if you're not going on holiday to South America.

John Davies, author of 'Ticket to Tewkesbury', etc

We enjoyed this book because it conveys the reality of travel in these countries and the everyday issues facing the traveller. Too many travel books tend to present a 'tourist board' image of a location which is very different from the practical experience of the average visitor. Problems, hiccups and the unexpected help one to understand and appreciate a country much more. This book is a real journal of an exciting and challenging venture and not just a 'puff' for the South American tourist industry. Well worth reading.

Brian and Margaret Ludlow

Valerie Astill

Temples and Tacos

This fascinating trip consisted of so much more than learning about ancient civilisations such as the Aztecs, Zapotecs and Mayans and seeing the remains of their once great cities. Whether travelling by coach, visiting a remote site by five-seater aeroplane or travelling upriver by boat, the journey itself was part of the adventure.

However, it was the discovery that many Indians still practised ancient customs, plus unexpected events such as an erupting volcano, falling rocks and animals invading the bedroom at night that made this journey through Mexico, Guatemala and Belize so memorable.

In this insightful book meet the priests and the natives and find out why the Zapotecs felt it was an honour to be selected for human sacrifice and even delighted at the thought that they may be chosen. Also discover why a bottle of Coca Cola was revered by the Indians and many other bizarre traditions and beliefs!

Pneuma Springs Publishing

An insightful account for the discerning traveller.

publishedbestsellers.com

Valerie Astill's.....minutely detailed accounts of visits to ancient Aztec, Mayan and Zapotec sites give a vivid picture of people as well as places. Thanks to excellent guides, the Astills were able to learn much of the background of the sites they visited – some of it blood-curdling, as in Aztec human sacrifices to the Sun God when the victim's heart was cut out, still beating.

Joan Stephens, Leicester Mercury

For more information, visit www.valerieastill.co.uk